ATHLETICS AND THE LAW

Dr. Herb Appenzeller

Athletic Director
Guilford College
Greensboro, North Carolina

THE MICHIE COMPANY

Law Publishers

CHARLOTTESVILLE, VIRGINIA

TO MY MOTHER AND FATHER

IN LOVE ALWAYS

PREFACE

In 1970 I wrote *From the Gym to the Jury* which dealt with the legal aspects of pupil injuries in athletics and physical education. As a result of the interest in the topic, I had the opportunity to lecture at conferences, clinics, and workshops in many states.

At the various meetings, coaches, athletes, and administrators raised numerous questions concerning not only liability for injuries but every possible area of law and athletics.

Because of the unusual interest in athletic law and because litigation has become such a vital factor in the life of the athlete and coach, I have written *Athletics and the Law*.

In this book I have attempted to answer the inquiries that have posed problems to so many people. I have tried to present the material in a style that is legally sound and at the same time easy to comprehend.

The chapters include the trends in litigation, disruptive behavior, the changing attitude of the court toward married athletes, training rules and good conduct codes. They include the ever-present problem of athletic travel, the changing role of women's athletics, the role of state athletic associations with their diverse rules, federal legislation, a potpourri of miscellaneous cases that continue to plague schoolmen and the area of due process. A final chapter offers conclusions that sum up the material in the ten chapters.

At the end of chapters two through ten is a short section entitled "In My Opinion." In this section, I freely comment on the material in the chapter, using my experience as a participant, coach, teacher, and administrator.

I am grateful to James Gifford who read the manuscript and offered many valuable suggestions. I appreciate the effort of Henry Semmler who made recommendations regarding content and style in the book. Special appreciation is due Ann Johnson who secured many documents and court cases that are important to the book. I am indebted to Sheila J. Kendall for the many hours she devoted in typing the manuscript and to Duke Hilliard who did the illustrations in a clever and interesting style.

As always I am grateful to my family for their patience, enthusiasm and inspiration.

Herb Appenzeller

Greensboro, North Carolina
March, 1975

CONTENTS

1. The Law and the Locker Room

Let us not in seeking the perfect,
destroy the good.[1]

A new day has arrived in both athletics and physical education. Interest in athletics at all levels, from little league to professional play, has reached unprecedented proportions. This is the era of crowded stadiums, Monday night televised football, instant replay, multi-million dollar contracts and record participation.

On the other hand, law and athletics are becoming synonymous as lawsuits are filed in alarming and record-breaking numbers. Athletes in locker rooms discuss such things as personal rights, due process, equal protection, and the guarantees of the First, Fourth, Fifth, Ninth and Fourteenth Amendments. Judges and juries are called upon to consider every possible type of case and school officials are becoming frustrated over the claims and contentions brought forward by athletes, coaches, and spectators alike.

Several court cases illustrate the latest trends in

athletic litigation and the attitude of the courts toward these claims.

Ohio State played nationally-ranked Minnesota in a highly publicized basketball game in January, 1972.[2] Pre-game interest reached a fever pitch as Big Ten leadership, national prestige, and intercollegiate rivalry made the game important to sport fans everywhere.

Unfortunately, the score of the game became lost to other events as a fierce and bloody brawl erupted that left a nation of sport-lovers in shock. Charges and counter-charges were leveled on all sides, but the damage to intercollegiate athletics was profound.

Wayne Duke, the Commissioner of the Big Ten Conference hastily conducted an investigation into the fight. Big Ten regulations place an obligation on the individual school to conduct an investigation and administer punishment if needed. The Committee on Intercollegiate Athletics at the host University of Minnesota looked into the facts, and as a result, suspended Ronald Behagen and Marvin Taylor from further intercollegiate basketball competition for the remainder of the season.

Three days later, the Commissioner met with the athletic directors of the Conference to consider the University's disciplinary action. The group refused to accept the Committee's penalty for the explosive incident, and imposed an additional punishment by denying the basketball players the privilege of daily practice with the team.

Behagen and Taylor charged the group of athletic directors with a violation of their right of due process since the group made their decision without giving them a hearing. Their claim was upheld by the District Court in Minnesota. The court decreed that "big-time" athletics in colleges today often adds a different dimension to sports that at times overshadows the educational program. The new element — money! The court's response is a novel one in a day when educators agree that education, not athletics, takes precedence in the life of a student-athlete. The court answered this philosophy by observing that:

> in these days when juniors in college are able to suspend their formal educational training in exchange for multi-million contracts to turn professional, this court takes judicial notice of the fact that, to many, the chance to display their athletic prowess in college stadiums and arenas throughout the country is more in economic terms than the chance to get a college education.

The Minnesota District Court disallowed the athletic directors' decision to prohibit practice for Behagen and Taylor. The District Court did, however, uphold the University's Committee in denying the players further basketball competition. It warned the Committee that an undue delay in conducting the full investigation would be looked upon by the court as punitive action and a violation of the athletes' rights.

E. C. Bolmeier, outstanding school law authority, describes Civil Rights as:

> those rights which pertain to an individual by virtue of his citizenship or residence in a community or state. Whereas natural rights are considered to exist outside of law and independent of government, civil rights exist under law guaranteed by federal and state constitutions. Civil rights include personal freedoms such as religious liberty, freedom of speech, security against unreasonable search and seizure, the guaranty against self-incrimination, the right to trial by jury, and the right to equal protection of the laws.[3]

Unlike many athletes, faculty members have long been aware of their right of due process and constitutional guarantees. It is not surprising, therefore, that a tenured assistant professor of political science appealed his firing by the University of Missouri's Chancellor.[4]

Patrick Dougherty protested the participation of the University band and football team in a parade for the "Veiled Prophet Order." Dougherty sent a letter to the Chancellor describing the organization as racist. He deplored the University's sanction of the parade and he read the letter to his class and then sent a copy to the local press.

To draw attention to his protest, Dougherty shaved his head and went on a hunger strike. He followed the band and football team to St. Louis and marched alongside carrying a picture of the late Martin Luther King. Suddenly, on impulse, he threw himself on the street in front of the marching band members and was immediately arrested by the St. Louis police for disturbing the peace.

Dougherty's departmental dean suspended him with pay until a full inquiry into the incident could be held. Two faculty committees met and recommended his reinstatement. The president refused to adopt their recommendations and fired Dougherty with a 3-2 approval by the Board of Curators. The District Court in Missouri affirmed his firing.

The United States Appeals Court took the opposite view of the president's action. It reasoned that the University had the right to fire the professor for his conduct during the parade, but asserted that Dougherty's rights were impaired when the University "punished him as well for writing and publicly releasing the letter."

On the secondary level, many teachers and coaches are beginning to sue school boards when their contracts are terminated. A 1973 case is pending that is typical of the latest trend that is developing in such situations.

Wayne Hoover had coached for 21 years in North Carolina. For eight years he served as director of physical education, social studies teacher, basketball and golf coach.[5] When the Lexington School Board fired him by a 3-2 vote, Hoover filed a $150,000 lawsuit against the school board, superintendent, and principal. Hoover charged the defendants with denying him his right of due process.

After Hoover was called before the Board to discuss his coaching ability, not his teaching record, the Board voted 2-2-1 to rehire him. The school attorney interpreted the tie as favorable to Hoover, but Robert Morgan, North Carolina's Attorney General, considered it a mandate for dismissal.

A final hearing was instituted and Hoover was offered the position of "probationary teacher," which he rejected. He insisted that he qualified for the position of "career teacher" due to his length of service.

His case will be heard by the U. S. Middle District Court in Greensboro, North Carolina.

Court injunctions have even dipped down into little league baseball.[6] A court order halted a little league championship game in Raleigh, North Carolina, over a ruling made by an umpire. The program's director wearily decried such action and commented that possibly future tournaments would be discontinued since "there is too much pressure for the 10-12 year-old boys when something like this happens."

Two girls in Michigan challenged the school board's rule prohibiting them from interscholastic competition.[7] The Circuit Court upheld the lower court's judgment in part, but modified it by allowing girls to compete in "non-contact" sports. The court emphasized that a rule that prevented girls from playing on teams with boys deprived them of their rights under the Equal Protection Clause of the Fourteenth Amendment.

The above cases are a typical sampling of recent litigation as plaintiffs charge discrimination, based on violations of constitutional guarantees. Since the inception of the Civil Rights Act, injunctions against school boards are common.

This fact prompted a Pennsylvania district court to remark that: [8]

> Courts are flooded with claims allegedly arising under the Civil Rights Act. Every act, every administrative decision of every state and local official is today threatened by federal litigation. This extends to every organization or institution that receives some financial support from state or local government sources.

In response to the proliferation of cases, the Court

in *King-Smith v. Aaron* [9] pleaded for reasonableness regarding Civil Rights litigation, by stating:

> if state and local governments are to remain viable instruments and not become administrative agencies of the federal court system, there must remain some avenues by which local concerns are solved locally through the democratic process. Using the Civil Rights Act as a vehicle to threaten every exercise of discretion in matters legitimately within the area of a state's competence is not the purpose of this grant of jurisdiction to the federal courts.

The sums of money sought for damages in the courts today have grown to enormous amounts. P. K. Peterson, an insurance executive, talked candidly about the rise of damage awards when he predicted that: [10]

> the former limits for which liability policies were written are no longer regarded as adequate. Courts are taking judicial notice of dollar depreciation, and verdicts that would have been considered excessive ten years ago are no longer regarded as sufficient to compensate an injured person for loss sustained as the result of an injury.

For example, a Superior Court in Chatham, New Jersey awarded Stanley Miller $1,216,000 for injuries he received in a 1962 physical education class.[11] Although Judge Elden Mills sympathized with the injured boy, he reduced the amount of the award to $335,140.00. Mills asserted that "it is not the purpose of the award to enrich him but to reasonably compensate him for his injuries, his pain and suffering, both in the past and the future." Mills took in consideration all the expenses, past, present, and future and gave his reasons for reducing the award by stating:

> However, let's look at it another way. If the award of $1,180,000 was invested after the payment of counsel fees, what would it return per year? Let's assume one-third would go for counsel fees and expenses or better than $787,000 would be left, at three per cent the income would be $23,633 per year. Could not careful management of the fund increase the principal? The net result could be that Stanley could live a normal life and leave as an estate more than he received for his injuries.

If Peterson is correct, and awards will not be reduced as in the past, it will be interesting to follow the progress of a recent San Francisco case. Kelley Niles, a thirteen-year-old boy, received $4,025,000 for injuries he sustained in a playground fight.[12] Niles was hit on the head with a bat during an argument. A doctor and medical crew at Mt. Zion Hospital examined Niles and released him. Several hours later, Niles was rushed to the hospital where he underwent extensive brain surgery. Recently his lawyer described him as having "an alert mind in a useless body."

Niles' award of over four million dollars is the highest individual award in United States history.

Will the court reduce this record-breaking award or will the prediction of a new trend in damages hold true?

Peterson also explained the huge cost of awards by commenting that: [13]

> the decreased value of the dollar has been recognized by appellate courts in refusing to reduce verdicts, which formerly might have been considered excessive. Claims running into enormous sums are constantly being paid. The public is becoming liability-minded, and rare indeed is the accident where some liability suit is not filed as a result of the accident.

The tremendous cost involved in lawsuit awards has been described as the "injury industry." [14]

Three recent cases indicate the exorbitant amounts sought for damages.

David LeBright, a member of the Raleigh-Durham Baseball Club, sued the organization for $200,000 for directing him to play while injured.[15] LeBright insisted that his career, which was promising, was curtailed. Further, he testified that the Club failed to pay his hospital bills as promised.

A University of Kentucky athlete became a quadraplegic from injuries sustained while playing football. He sued the University and the National Collegiate Athletic Association for $10 million.[16]

In 1975 the parents of a 10-year-old boy who almost drowned during a summer camp at Wake Forest University have instituted a suit against the University and nine of its employees for $23.1 million.[17]

Clearly, damage suits are ending in many instances in astronomical amounts that seem to grow unheeded.

It is important to know the various categories of the court system in which school men are involved. The authors of *Public School Law* reveal the judicial structure by explaining that: [18]

> the power for the operation of the public educational system originates with the Constitutional delegation of power for the legislature to provide for a system of education. *With legislative enactments providing the basis for public school law*, it then becomes the role of the courts, through litigation, to interpret the will of the legislature. The combination of constitutions, statutes, and court or case law form the primary legal foundation on which public schools are based.[19]

The courts are separated by various duties that include:

(1) *Courts of General Jurisdiction*

These courts are referred to as district or circuit courts with the responsibility of handling all matters except those referred to special courts.

(2) *Courts of Special Jurisdiction*

Litigation that deals with large numbers of cases is handled here. The most common courts include "probate courts, domestic courts, and juvenile courts."

(3) *Small Claims Courts*
As the name implies, lawsuits that involve small amounts of money are settled here.

(4) *Appellate Courts*
All states have appellate courts that hear appeals from trial courts. These courts are often called the Supreme Court or Court of Appeals. (Larger states such as New York and California may have intermediate **courts.**)

Frequently, litigation concerning athletics or physical education goes to the federal courts when the issue raises constitutional questions. The United States federal court system includes "district courts, courts of appeals, special federal courts, and the Supreme Court." [20]

Each state has at least one district court and often there are two or more. The Federal District Court is empowered to handle various types of litigation such as:

(1) cases between citizens of different states.
(2) cases involving litigation of federal statutes or the federal Constitution.

The District Court is usually a one judge court but "in cases of injunction against the enforcement of a state or federal statute, a three-judge court is required." [21] A District Court decision can be appealed to the Federal Court of Appeals and occasionally to the Supreme Court.

In the federal judicial system, there are eleven appellate courts in each of the eleven judicial circuits. In the 8th Circuit District, for example, North Dakota, South Dakota, Nebraska, Minnesota, Iowa, Missouri and Arkansas are included.[22]

Athletic and physical education cases go to the courts above. If a state or federal statute is in question, the plaintiff may obtain a "writ of certiorari" which, if viewed by the court to be valid, may proceed to the highest court of the land, the Supreme Court, from which there is no appeal.[23]

Finally, it is well to remember that each case is decided on its own merits. While certain principles may be established as well as precedents, the human element of the jury, the powerful persuasion of a lawyer, and other factors make decisions unpredictable at times. It has been said that:

> the rule of law is also the rule of men. Legal disputes involve conflicts between people; lawyers and judges, after all, are men possessed of opinions, prejudices and passions. Their arguments and conclusions will reflect not only the application of a legal principle to a particular set of facts; they will mirror their social attitudes and philosophies, as well as personal unspoken judgments on the merits of the case before them.[24]

1. Homer Babbidge, PROCEEDINGS OF THE THIRD ANNUAL NACDA CONVENTION, Cleveland, Ohio, June, 1968.
2. Behagen v. Intercollegiate Conference of Faculty Representatives, 346 F. Supp. 602 (D. Minn. 1972).
3. E. C. BOLMEIER, LEGAL LIMITS OF AUTHORITY OVER THE PUPIL, The Michie Co., Charlottesville, Va., 1970.
4. Dougherty v. Walker, 349 F. Supp. 629 (W.D. Mo. 1972).

5. Greensboro Daily News, August 14, 1973.
6. The Fayetteville Times, July 28, 1973.
7. Morris v. Michigan State Bd. of Educ., No. 72-1578, U.S. Ct. App. (6th Cir. 1973).
8. NOLPE NOTES, National Organization of Legal Problems in Education (SLQ 3Q 70).
9. King-Smith v. Aaron, 317 F. Supp. 164 (W.D. Pa. 1970).
10. P. K. Peterson, *Modern Approaches to Liability and Insurance*, PROCEEDINGS OF THE THIRD ANNUAL NACDA CONVENTION, Cleveland, Ohio, June, 1968, at 50.
11. Miller v. Cloidt & Bd. of Educ. of the Borough of Chatham, No. L7241-62 (N.J. Super. Ct. 1964).
12. Charleston News and Courier, Fall, 1972.
13. P. K. Peterson, *supra* note 10.
14. *Id.*
15. Greensboro Daily News, August 12, 1973.
16. New v. University of Kentucky & NCAA, USDC #8077, Ohio, 1973.
17. Winston-Salem Journal, January 11, 1975.
18. ALEXANDER, KERN, CORNS, RAY, McCANN, WALTER, PUBLIC SCHOOL LAW, West Publishing Co., St. Paul, Minn., 1969.
19. *Id.*
20. *Id.* at 9.
21. *Id.* at 10.
22. *Id.*
23. *Id.*
24. *Id.* at 2.

2. Penalty Call!

*They cannot be adults when they choose to be
and juveniles when that course of action
appeals to them more.*[1]

The sit-ins at the dime store lunch counters in Greensboro, North Carolina, started a new era in student protest. The protests of the 1950's consisted of petitions, resolutions, editorials and letters in school publications. These protests continued into the 1960's but students, aided by professional agitators, added a new dimension, violence. Molotov cocktails, barricaded doors, chemical sprays, occupied buildings and hostages became common words on college campuses and even spread to the secondary schools.

In April, 1969, the extreme form of protest was reached when a janitor at the University of Santa Barbara picked up a package outside the Faculty Club and died when a bomb inside the package exploded. During the same year, a secretary at Pomona College lost several fingers, the sight in one eye, and underwent painful plastic surgery, when a bomb exploded in a faculty mailbox.[2]

In 1970, the F.B.I., in a special report on campus disruption, found that the damages exceeded $1.5 million.[3] No area of campus life escaped the violent protests and nonviolent demonstrations of the 1960's. In 1968-69, over 145 institutions of higher learning were plagued with violence, while more than 400 institutions experienced nonviolent protests.

Bayer and Astin define violent protests as those involving the "burning of a building, damage to a building or furnishings, destruction of files, records or papers, campus march, picketing, or a rally with physical violence and the injury or death of any person."[4] They classified nonviolent disruptive protests as the "occupation of a building, barring of entrance to a building, holding officials captive, interruption of classes, speeches or meetings, general campus strike or boycott of classes or a school function."[5]

Athletic programs have been challenged by boycotts, take-over of facilities, bomb threats, and other methods of protest. Many athletic directors, unaware of the legal aspects of campus disruption, have become vulnerable to the tactics of student activists. It has been said that "activists on many campuses frequently take advantage of the administrator's lack of knowledge to get concessions that have little relation to either law or education." [6]

The threat of disruption remains ever present but the 1970's appear to be headed back to the style of protest that was popular in the 1950's. As long as violence can erupt, however, it is well to consider previous situations with the attitude of the court emphasized. If the rights of the institution and the student are to be protected, the administrator needs to know what rights are in order. [7]

Disruption Cases with Implications for Athletics

Athletic directors are troubled by the threat of a take-over of athletic fields and facilities or the barring of entrances, interruption of programs or games by militant protestors. The picture is fairly clear, as evidenced by recent court decisions.

In most disruption cases, students often complain that they have been denied the rights guaranteed them by the First Amendment; the right to assemble and free speech. The courts consistently maintain that institutions have the right to set reasonable rules to govern their campuses and students have a responsibility to observe these rules. [8]

The court also emphasizes that in cases of

disruption with force, the constitutional rights of
free speech and assembly are not violated.[9]

Justice Arthur Goldberg stated the court's position on disruption when he said:

> We emphatically reject the notion that the
> first and fourteenth amendments afford
> the same kind of freedom to those who
> would communicate ideas by conduct such
> as patrolling, marching, and picketing on
> streets and highways as these amendments
> afford to those who communicate ideas by
> pure speech.

Justice Goldberg added, "the state may impose
reasonable restrictions on time, place, duration
and manner." [10]

Supreme Court Justice Abe Fortas added weight
to Justice Goldberg's opinions when he predicted
that "demonstrators lose their Constitutional protection if the participants engage in violence."
He also voiced his opinion that "noisy conduct
alone may justify restrictions in the interest of
preserving peace and quiet." [11]

The Solicitor General of the United States in a
speech in 1968 cautioned would-be activists that:

> Schools today are confronted with the
> delicate decision as to when to invoke the
> law in an effort to stop activism. If violence
> is resulting to property or physical harm,
> they have little choice but to use whatever
> tools the law gives. If the demonstration is
> merely in the noise and nuisance area, they
> may be willing to give time for the
> presentation of a point of view and attempt
> to negotiate. But if negotiations fail,

ultimately the schools will have to take
actions to abate the noise and nuisance. [12]

An interesting example of these sentiments took
place at Fort Collins, Colorado in 1970, when
Colorado State University officials faced an
explosive situation. A group of students planned to
demonstrate outside the gymnasium before a
basketball game between Colorado State University
and Brigham Young University. The students
charged Brigham Young University with racial
discrimination and wanted to draw attention to their
sentiments by peaceful protest. They applied for,
and were granted permission, by University
officials, to conduct an orderly protest.

At halftime when the Pom Pom girls from
Brigham Young were putting on a show, the
demonstrators came on the basketball court and
interrupted the performance. A fight broke out
between an employee, who was sweeping the floor,
and some of the demonstrators. Police from the
campus and City of Fort Collins alertly prevented
additional trouble. During the melee, someone threw
a firebrand onto the basketball court and a
photographer was hit with a piece of steel on the
head. The situation was described as one in which
the:

> tempers of many of the spectators
> (including the tempers of the overwhelming
> majority of the students in attendance)
> became short, and the rage of the crowd at
> the unauthorized interruption of the
> halftime activities and delay of play of the

second half became dangerously apparent.
The situation was tense, and panic or a riot
was more than a mere possibility.

The court viewed films of the incident and
commended the outstanding work and ability of the
police in handling such a dangerous situation.

After such an explosive situation, the Colorado
State University officials drew up a regulation to
prevent future protests that could endanger the lives
of spectators and participants alike. Several parts of
the regulation stated in essence that the University
did not object to peaceful protest by students as long
as the participants respected the property rights and
safety of others. It requested groups planning
demonstrations to contact school authorities in
advance. Violation of the regulations would lead to
suspension or dismissal from the University.

A group of students immediately challenged the
February 6 regulation and stated their intention to
test it. The part of the regulation they objected to
pointed out that the institution did not want
interference with the facilities of a scheduled
athletic event.

Several weeks after the regulation was adopted, a
wrestling match was held with the opponent once
again being Brigham Young University. A group of
students led by Robert Evans obtained permission to
peacefully demonstrate outside the gymnasium but
were denied permission to protest inside the
gymnasium where the wrestling match was held. As
a result of the refusal by the University to grant
permission to demonstrate inside the gymnasium, a

lawsuit was instituted by the students, against the officials of the school.

The District Court in Colorado reviewed previous cases that related, in principle, to the present litigation. The various ideas expressed in the previous cases interpreted the mood of the court in such disruptive situations.

The court looked at *Buttny v. Smiley*,[13] in which Chief Judge Arraj predicted things that later came true in the *Tinker v. Des Moines* case. Arraj agreed that the doctrine of *In Loco Parentis* was outmoded and did not fit the times for college students. He also believed that schools could not continue to regulate the conduct of students off campus. He did feel, however, that when disruptive conduct took place, the school officials could take disciplinary action. Arraj summed up the attitude of the court by strongly stating:

> We do not subscribe to the notion that a citizen surrenders his civil rights upon enrollment as a student in a university. As a corollary to this, enrollment does not give him a right to immunity nor special consideration, and certainly it does not give him the right to violate the constitutional rights of others.[14]

The court then considered *Tinker* which has become a landmark decision regarding the display of symbols as a method of expressing dissent.[15] In *Tinker* the school officials adopted a policy prohibiting the wearing of armbands to protest the Vietnam War. The court subsequently overruled the school policy as a violation of the first amendment rights of students. The court argued that "a mere desire to avoid the discomfort and unpleasantness that always accompany an unpopular viewpoint" was not cause enough to deny such freedom of expression. It might be well to point out that in the *Tinker* case, the school permitted the wearing of various symbols without penalty. Only the black armbands were subject to the policy rule and suspension.

The Colorado District Court observed that, in the present case being tried, the regulation was not directed against a particular "school of thought" but was designed to handle all "previously scheduled activities." It then quoted the dicta in *Hammond v. South Carolina State College* [16] that clearly articulated the question of student responsibility by pointing out that:

> college attendance, whether it be a right or privilege, very definitely entails responsibility. This is fundamental. It rests upon the fact that the student is approaching maturity. His elementary and secondary education is behind him. He already knows, or should know, the basics of decent conduct, of nonviolence, and of respect for the rights of others. He already knows, or should know, that destruction of property, threats to others, frightening passersby and intrusions upon their rights or travel are unacceptable, if not illegal, and are not worthy of one who would pursue knowledge at the college level. These plaintiffs are no longer children.

The court in the *Hammond* case continued by explaining:

> Let there be no misunderstanding as to our precise holding. We do not hold that any college regulation, however loosely framed, is necessarily valid. We do not hold that a school has the authority to require a student to discard any constitutional right when he matriculates. We do hold that a college has the inherent power to promulgate rules and regulations; that is the inherent power properly to discipline; that it has the power appropriately to protect itself and its property; that it may expect that its students adhere to generally accepted standards of conduct.

Finally, the Colorado Court made several key points that are noteworthy when it concluded that:

(1) School regulations and policy statements **need not meet all of the standards of certainty required of criminal** statutes.

(2) They must be reasonable. They must be understandable.

(3) Students rightfully seeking enforcement of their constitutional rights must accept the duties of responsible citizens.

(4) They must not confuse their constitutionally protected right of free speech with an illusive and nonexistent right to violently disrupt. They cannot be adults when they choose to be and juveniles when that course of conduct appeals to them more.

(5) University officials are charged with

the responsibility of conducting a well
ordered institution, and in carrying out
their responsibility they have not only
the right but the duty to adopt and
enforce such policies and regulations
. . . to be required by the factual
situation with which they are faced.
(6) The constitutional right of freedom of
speech is the right to dissent, but it is
not the unfettered right to disrupt by
force and violence, and it is not the
unqualified right to interfere with the
rights and safety of others.

Not only did the court feel that the action taken
by the officials at Colorado State University was
justified but actually required by the incendiary
conditions that existed. It also felt that it was
unfortunate that the actions "of a few misguided"
students made such a regulation necessary when the
majority of students were responsible citizens.

The attitude of the court upheld the role of the
administrator in establishing policy and formulating
rules for the operation of the school. The point that is
made, over and over, is that while rules are valid
they must be reasonable and understandable. These
are the essential factors.

While the courts have been as specific as possible
regarding rules, exceptions seem to be present
always. One case that clouds the issue is *Soglin v.
Kauffman* [17] in which a group of Wisconsin
University students prevented other students from
attending classes. The protestors did not want the
recruiters for the Dow Chemical Company to seek

potential employees since that company made products used in the Vietnam War. The students involved in the protest were suspended on charges of "misconduct." The University officials felt that all rules did not need to be specific in nature and relied on *Esteban v. Central Missouri College* [18] to support this belief. In the *Esteban* case, the court held that higher education should not set up detailed codes of prohibited conduct. Yet, in the *Soglin* case, the court questioned the University's use of the word "misconduct" and finally concluded that it was too broad and vague. In *Soglin* the court failed to uphold the University's action in suspending the students who engaged in the demonstration.

While the court may choose to rule that a regulation is too vague or broad, it appears that it will support regulations that are reasonable and understandable. It will support institutions that set the time and place of campus meetings and require advance reservations for the use of areas or buildings on campus.

Regulating Student Protest

The University of Wyoming was scheduled to play Brigham Young University in football on October 18, 1969.[19] The day before the game, a group of fourteen black athletes asked their football coach, Lloyd Eaton, to discuss the Brigham Young protest with them. At the time they entered the coach's office, each of the fourteen was dressed in civilian clothes with black armbands. Their coach dismissed them from the team, citing a team rule that prohibited demonstrations. The fourteen players instituted a lawsuit against their football coach, athletic director, president, and trustees of the University. They sought damages of $75,000 for each plaintiff. The plaintiffs insisted that their dismissal was:

(1) a deprivation of their right to peaceably demonstrate under the Constitution of the United States.

(2) without a proper hearing or notice of any charges and without an opportunity to present evidence in their behalf.

(3) a violation of their rights under the First, Ninth, and Fourteenth Amendments of the Federal Constitution and various provisions of the Wyoming Constitution.

(4) intended to penalize them for exercising such rights, and to compel conformance to undefined concepts of personal behavior set by the Coach, the Athletic Director, the University President and the Trustees.

(5) a vague and over-broad requirement with a chilling effect on the exercise of the First and Ninth Amendments.

The defendants answered the charges by stating that the action taken by the University did not violate any constitutional rights of the plaintiffs. Their scholarships were not withdrawn although the fourteen athletes were alleged to threaten that they would not return until the football coach was dismissed. The defendants vigorously argued that if they permitted the players to wear armbands against Brigham Young University, they, in fact, would:

> have acted as State officers and agents contrary to the First Amendment prohibition against State establishment of any religion and its guarantee for free exercise of religion, and like provisions of the Wyoming Constitution.

The players claimed that their dismissal from the team denied them the opportunity to develop their skills and obtain the possibility of professional football scouts seeing them during the 1969 season. As a result this "has caused them emotional and mental stress and anxiety."

The court considered the facts that were presented and reviewed the decision for dismissal by the District Court. It agreed that the District Court acted properly when it dismissed the case regarding the State of Wyoming's regulations regarding religious neutrality and the immunity of state officers but ruled that the case needed further consideration regarding "such close and delicate constitutional questions" and remanded it back for "further proceedings."

Athletic directors and school administrators receive considerable criticism when spectators at athletic events refuse to stand for the National Anthem or pledge to the flag.

In December, 1969, Judge Orrin G. Rudd ruled on a case in which three New York students refused to stand or repeat the pledge of allegiance to the flag.[20]

The three students involved felt that the school officials did not have the authority to ask them to leave the classroom because they would not participate in the pledge.

The students stated that the words "with liberty and justice for all" did not apply to them and that they would be violating their conscience by repeating them. They argued strongly that their refusal to repeat the pledge was a right guaranteed to them by the Constitution of the United States.

Judge Rudd answered critics who feel that school officials and athletic directors should remove dissenters from the stadium, classroom and athletic field when he ruled that the:

> students had a right of silent protest by remaining seated and that the right included the privilege of expressing themselves in their own way as long as they didn't disrupt the school or infringe on the rights of others. School officials will have to prove disruption or infringement of others' rights before discipline can take place.

IN MY OPINION

The courts have a history of deferring policymaking and management of athletics to those who conduct the programs. When policies are fair and reasonable, there is little to fear from the courts. When programs are run arbitrarily and rules are devised that are unreasonable, then, and only then, will the court take over. In too many instances, school administrators hesitate to take action because they are afraid of a lawsuit. This hesitation often leads to tragic incidents that could have been avoided if action had been taken immediately. Most administrators tend to give student activists more rights than the average citizen receives because they lack the knowledge of legal rights.

Public opinion has caused state legislators to enact into law many statutes that have been termed unrealistic and unworkable. Still others, while possibly aiding administrators, may be vague and too broad.

Many athletic directors and coaches continue to live with outdated rules because they will not accept change. The courts support educators who try to operate a school program and reject repeated cries of violated rights. The courts expect administrators to take action when violence is imminent and the safety of people is threatened. Students are not given immunity just because they attend school nor do they have the right to violate the constitutional guarantees of others.

Yet, too often, administrators try to avoid embarrassment to their institutions by "sweeping under the rug" campus violations. Narcotic agents in many communities will tell you confidentially that the least cooperative people, in curbing the drug problem, are the school officials. After World War II under the "in loco parentis" concept, a student would be sent home immediately for a drinking violation. The student who drank drew the righteous indignation of the administrator while the pervert and thief were often sheltered for campus rehabilitation by some still unidentified educational process that was supposed to be the panacea to all problems except alcohol and murder. The wise administrator realizes that such action creates a dangerous double standard that can divide and alienate both students and community from the school.

Robert Morgan, North Carolina's Attorney General, in a presentation to the North Carolina Coaches Association said that too often administrators and others in positions of authority in the school create problems because they are afraid to take immediate action.[21] Quick and timely action could often prevent needless disruption but school officials are so often afraid of consequences because the threat of litigation hangs over them so that they delay action and situations become complex and destructive that could have been avoided with prompt action. "Take prudent but swift action and we will back you at the highest state level," advised Morgan.

The court has said that the school officials have the obligation to create a climate for learning at their institutions. It has repeatedly stated that a student cannot hinder the educational process of others through disruptive behavior.

To sum up the attitude of the court, several guidelines may be helpful that relate to disruption procedures:

(1) Adopt policies that are applicable to your institution.

(2) Involve all factions of your school in the construction of policies.

(3) Adopt rules that are specific and not vague or too broad. Keep fairness and reasonableness as the guiding feature.

(4) Publish and announce the rules and regulations in advance.

(5) Punish all violations. Do not protect criminal action.

(6) Have a plan ready to go into action before disruption takes place.

1. A. FLATH, ATHLETICS IN AMERICA (Oregon State University Press, 1972), at 84.

2. O. S. SIMS, JR., NEW DIRECTIONS IN CAMPUS LAW ENFORCEMENT: A HANDBOOK FOR ADMINISTRATORS (The University of Georgia Center for Continuing Education, 1970).

3. *Id.*

4. BAYER AND ASTIN, VIOLENCE AND DISRUPTION ON U.S. CAMPUS 1968-69, Educational Record.

5. *Id.*

6. Wentworth, *College's Facing Test on Justice,* Washington Post, September 7, 1969, at BL col. 5.

7. BAYER AND ASTIN, *supra* note 4 at 13.

8. Zanders v. Louisiana State Bd. of Educ., 281 F. Supp. 747 (W.D. La. 1968).

9. State v. Greenwald, 265 A.2d 720 (Conn. 1969).

10. Cox v. Louisiana, 379 U.S. 536 (1965).

11. Brown v. Louisiana, 383 U.S. 131 (1966).

12. Evans v. State Bd. of Agriculture, 325 F. Supp. 1353 (D. Colo. 1971).

13. Buttny v. Smiley, 281 F. Supp. 280 (D. Colo. 1968).

14. Tinker v. Des Moines Independent Community School Dist., 393 U.S. 503 (1969).

15. *Id.*

16. Hammond v. South Carolina State College, 272 F. Supp. 947 (D.S.C. 1967).

17. Soglin v. Kauffman, 295 F. Supp. 978 (W.D. Wis. 1968).
18. Esteban v. Central Missouri State College, 415 F.2d 1077 (8th Cir. 1969).
19. Williams v. Eaton, 443 F.2d 422 (10th Cir. 1971).
20. NOLPE NOTES, Vol. 5, No. 1, at 2, January, 1970.
21. Robert Morgan, Speech to North Carolina High School Coaches Ass'n, August, 1973, Greensboro, N.C.

3. More than the X's and O's

X O

O O O O

X X

X

Coaches are the sole executioners of justice.[1]

Good conduct codes for athletes have changed drastically in the last ten years. Coaches and administrators have frequently varied in their approach to training rules, dress codes, and married athletes. In many instances such codes have caused dissension and animosity on a team, in a school, or even in a community. While differences existed in the past, today the opposition to previously accepted codes are often litigated in the courts.

Not only do regulations differ among coaches and administrators, they are in conflict among the courts. Among 104 cases in which hairstyles have been litigated 58 were decided in favor of the school officials while 46 upheld the student.[2]

Justice Hugo Black indicated that the courts are losing their patience over the issue of hairstyles and the crowded court dockets that are filled with such cases. Justice Black recommends that local school authorities handle the regulation of appearance, dress and similar codes and not the federal courts.[3]

The main issue appears to be whether the length of hair is disruptive to the operation of an athletic team. School officials usually receive the support of the court when they can prove that a particular hairstyle is essential for team morale and the safety of the participant.

When the regulation is vague or indefinite the individual is usually favored by the court. Certain guidelines have been set by the courts for school boards to follow, such as:

(1) The restraint imposed by its regulations must rationally relate to the enhancement of the educational function,

(2) The public benefits produced must outweigh the consequent impairment of the students' constitutional rights, and

(3) There can be no alternatives "less subversive" of those rights.[4]

The court has upheld cases for the schools when it was satisfied that the rules were not unreasonable, arbitrary or capricious but were related instead to safety, discipline, athletics, and teaching good grooming.[5]

One of the most controversial cases took place in California in which the plaintiffs readily admitted that the length of their hair violated a regulation set by the athletic department.[6] The regulation required each athlete to be neat and well groomed, clean shaven, with the hair kept off the collar and at a reasonable length. Any violation of the rule would bring suspension from that particular sport.

The athletes were members of the track team who believed that such a stringent rule was not necessary or reasonable for competition in track. The coaches at Redwood High School were interviewed and community feeling and controversy developed over the case. The coaches urged support of the rule because they believed it was important for team morale, spirit, and discipline.

The court upheld the athletic department's regulation and commented that each case needs to be considered on its own merit according to the background and setting of the situation. It found that "the record is barren of any evidence that this was an arbitrary and capricious decision."

Finally, the California Court supported its decision by stating that:

> in these parlous, troubled times when discipline in certain quarters appears to be an ugly word, it should not be considered unreasonable nor regarded as an impingement of constitutional preroga-tives, to require plaintiffs to bring them-selves within the spirit, purpose and in-tendments of the questioned rule.

A Vermont Court saw the issue in a different way.[7]

Steve Durham, Prentiss Smith and Paul Weber instituted a suit against the school officials at Brattleboro High School protesting a rule they felt was a violation of their constitutional rights.

Brattleboro High School had certain policies regulating certain extracurricular activities, such as athletics, that required a proper amount of sleep and the avoidance of "substances harmful to the human body and mind, such as alcohol, tobacco, and illicit drugs." The code also permitted guidelines that regulated the appearance of athletes during the seasons in which they participated in sports.

The athletic department set specific rules that were intended to promote good morale and team spirit. It specified among other things:

> For males, hair must be cut tapered in the back and on the sides of the head with no hair over the collar. Sideburns should be no lower than the earlobe and trimmed.

The boys, who were members of the tennis team, were reported to be very hard workers and eager to excel. They failed to comply with the athletic code and were dismissed from the team. The plaintiffs argued that no other member of the student body, nor participant in any other extracurricular activity at the school, was subject to such a code. They insisted that they could wear a sweat band to keep the hair out of their eyes since no one seemed to object to their hair in school.

An interesting comment was made during the trial regarding long hair and professional athletes:

> Billy Kidd, the world famous skier, Joe Pepitone and Ken Harrelson, two colorful and popular major league players, would be unable to make their teams. Ron Hill who won the Boston Marathon on April 19 of

this year would not even be permitted to
try out for the track team if he had to obey
the hair code.[8]

The Vermont Court reasoned that the important
factor in this case was the question of classification.
It felt that the regulation split the athletes at
Brattleboro High into two classes; those who obeyed
the code could participate in athletics while those
who disregarded it were suspended. The court also
stated that the argument about athletics as a "right"
or "privilege" did not relate to the question raised in
this case. The issue was the plaintiffs' contention
that discrimination was involved in their dismissal
over the length of their hair. The court agreed with
the charge of the plaintiffs by caustically saying
that:

> the Constitution does not stop at the public
> schools like a puppy waiting for its master,
> but instead it follows the student through
> the corridors, into the classroom and onto
> the athletic field.

The Vermont Court then relied on the comments
of several judges in previous hair cases who said:

(1) There can be little doubt that the
Constitution protects the freedoms to
determine one's own hairstyle and
otherwise to govern one's own personal
appearance.[9]

(2) There are few individual characteristics
more basic to one's personality and
image than the manner in which one
wears his hair.[10]

(3) Whether the hairstyles be regarded as

> evidence of conformity or of individuality, they are the most visible means of personality.[11]

(4) The cut of one's hairstyle is more fundamental than the type of clothing he wears. Garments can be changed at will whereas hair, once it is cut, has to remain constant for substantial periods of time.[12]

After reviewing the strong statements of previous courts, the Vermont Court concluded that there was no lack of discipline or performance on the Brattleboro High School Tennis Team because the players had long hair.

It then cautioned school officials to take notice that:

> it would be a bit frightening if a naked emphasis on conformity were to prevail in our public schools. Today's high school student will find that the world beyond his graduation is filled with pressures toward conformity. He will certainly not be deprived of the experience.

The court continued to warn of the dangers of conformity by adding:

> while conformity to reasonable rules of conduct is essential, conformity for its own sake is dangerous; and as the evidence indicated unrelated to performance in the sport of tennis. Standing alone, conformity per se is neither a reason nor a jurisdiction for the hair code in this case.

It then took exception to the "hair code" on the basis of uniformity by observing that:

> uniformity in hair length regulations between the various sports at Brattleboro Union High School was advanced as an independent reason for its application to the tennis squad. Here again, the only reason apparent from the evidence to justify uniformity is the value of uniformity for its own sake.

The Vermont Court met the issue head on with important dicta that certainly stand as a guideline to coaches and administrators alike. It ruled that the three boys should be reinstated without penalty immediately. As a concluding remark the court asked why:

> every sport could not have its own rules on hair length which would be reasonably related to performance in that particular sport.

David Long was a member of the Greenbrier East High School in West Virginia. His football coach required all the players to observe a "hair code" he set up.[13] The "hair code" applied throughout the entire school year and if a letter winner violated the rule he was denied both an invitation to the athletic banquet and also his award letter for football.

Long observed the "hair code" during the football season but let his hair grow long after it was over. His coach prohibited him from attending the banquet and refused to award him his letter, won in football that year. When the athlete appealed the action of his coach, the school authorities backed the coach and his decision.

A lawsuit was brought against the high school football coach and the school by the athlete and the U.S. District Court promptly dismissed the case. The plaintiff then appealed his case to the U.S. Court of Appeals, Fourth Circuit and they ruled in his favor by reversing the lower court's verdict.

The higher court cited *Massie v. Henry* [14] in which the court ruled that it was unconstitutional for a public school to force students to observe "hair codes." The Court of Appeals then concluded that the "doctrine of *Massie* is equally applicable to all school controlled activities. It extends to school athletic programs, as well as to school academic programs. Awards, properly earned in either field, cannot be used as instruments to enforce compliance with a 'hair code' for the enforcement of which there is no compelling necessity."

The Court of Appeals then emphasized that even if hygiene demanded short hair, there was no reason to enforce such a regulation after a season was over.

With this decision it is obvious that the court will seriously question a coach's action in denying an athlete an award which was won during a season for a violation after the season is over.

Training Rules

Many coaches set detailed rules regarding training policy that include the abstinence from certain drugs, including tobacco and alcohol, and the proper amount of sleep. Some coaches have liberal rules that are not as detailed or specific in nature.

In 1970 in New York, a coach revoked an athlete's varsity letters in football and track because he violated an established rule.[15] The rule prohibited an athlete from drinking at any time, during or after the season. The athlete in this case drank after the football and track seasons were over. The boy objected to the coach's action in taking back the letters he won in both sports. He admitted that he broke the rule but insisted that he was not given a proper hearing. The court supported the coach's right to revoke the letter since an established rule was violated. The court ruled, however, that the athlete should be given a hearing to discuss the matter with the school authorities.

In some instances today, athletes argue that they should be able to drink alcoholic beverages before a season begins as well as after it is over. In Ohio, a judge took the opposite attitude toward training rules when several basketball players were dismissed for pre-season drinking violations.[16] The boys tried to persuade the court that not only did the drinking take place out of season but the coach had never written the rules down or publicized them. The judge adopted a hard line which seems to be the exception today when he emphatically disagreed with the boys' arguments by stating that:

> Varsity sports, unlike intramurals, are a discretionary privilege and not a property right. . . . Coaches are the sole executioners of justice.

He then added:

> There is nothing that this court can take
> judicial notice of to indicate that politicians
> or bureaucrats, and I might add, judges, in
> control of scholastic athletics would
> perform, or could perform, the task as well
> as the school officials.

In another case involving drinking, five students
drank beer and then came to the gymnasium to
attend a high school dance.[17] The boys talked briefly
with the track coach who smelled the beer on their
breath. The track coach reported the incident to the
school's administrative assistant. The following day
when one of the boys came to track practice, he was
told by his coach that he was suspended from the
team for the remainder of the season. Another boy
who also drank beer that night was dropped from
the baseball squad for two games while a third boy,
guilty of the same offense, was dropped from the
junior varsity baseball team for the rest of the
season.

The administrative assistant placed all three of
the athletes on probation for the drinking incident.
The boys instituted a lawsuit against the school
officials because they thought the punishment was
unfair. They claimed that there were no written
rules that explained the policy on drinking, but
actually two separate, unwritten rules regarding
alcohol.

The athletic department had a policy which was
not written down that enabled each coach to handle
such violations as he saw fit. The principal had a

rule that placed violators on probation for one year. Such punishments were not made public to protect the reputation of individuals involved and this policy was virtually unknown to anyone except the principal.

The athletes argued that they realized that they would be punished by their individual coaches but they did not feel they would then be subject to additional punishment by the principal or his assistant.

Van Alstyne, who has written on student rights extensively, recommended that certain requisites be followed in disciplinary matters to protect the individual's rights. He listed:

  (1) Serious disciplinary action may not be taken in the absence of published rules which:
      a. Are not so vague that men of common intelligence must necessarily guess at its meaning and differ as to its application and
      b. Do not depend upon the qualified discretion of a particular administrator for their application.[18]

The court listened to the testimony and decided to uphold the school officials. It reasoned that the athletes knew that drinking would bring disciplinary action since the rule had been in effect, even though it was not written down. It also felt that the penalty was not severe enough to warrant full due process. While it preferred written rules and policy, the court accepted the fact that a school administrator could penalize a student who committed a violation without a written rule prohibiting the misconduct.

A final case is interesting for the attitude of the court is very definite in its support of school rules. A Georgia court made it clear that:

> Among the things a student is supposed to learn at school . . . is a sense of discipline. Of course, rules cannot be made by authorities for the sake of making them but they should possess considerable leeway in promulgating regulations for the proper conduct of students.[19]

It then defined its position on the responsibility of courts in such matters when it remarked:

> Courts should uphold them where there is any rational basis for the questioned rule. All that is necessary is a reasonable connection of the rule with the proper operation of the schools.

It concluded by giving future juries and judges advice on school cases when it observed that:

> Those who run the public schools should be the judges in such matters, not the courts. The quicker judges get out of the business of running schools the better . . . . Except in extreme cases the judgment of school officials should be final in applying a regulation to an individual case.

Married Athletes and Athletic Participation

For years school boards have attempted to limit teen-age marriages among high school students. School boards in many instances put restrictions against athletic participation for married athletes in the hope that this policy would be a deterrent to marriages.

The case of Jerry Kissick in the Garland Public High School in Texas was probably the landmark

case regarding a married athlete's attempt to participate in athletics.[20] The case and decision have been used by courts to guide them in similar situations.

The Garland Independent School District adopted a regulation that was designed to discourage teen-age marriages by restricting:

> married students or previously married
> students to be restricted wholly to
> classroom work; that they be barred
> from participating in athletics or other
> positions of honor. Academic honors

such as valedictorian and salutatorian are excepted.

Jerry Kissick was a high school football player who at the age of 16 married a 15-year-old girl. He testified that he planned to continue to play football with the hope of obtaining a college scholarship on his athletic ability. He charged the school district with a rule that was retroactive and thereby unreasonable and discriminatory.

It was brought out during the trial that participation in football counted toward credit in physical education which was part of the school curriculum. It was also revealed that the parents of junior and senior students in the school district had voted overwhelmingly in favor of a resolution favoring the marriage regulation. The court considered the fact that a year before the rule was put into effect 62 students were married. One-half of the group dropped at least 10 points in their academic grade average while 24 did not return to school or dropped out during the year.

The Texas Court voted to uphold the Garland School District's regulation. It reasoned that:

> Boards of Education rather than Courts are charged with the important and difficult duty of operating the public schools . . . The Court's duty, regardless of its personal views, is to uphold the Board's regulations unless they are generally viewed as being arbitrary and unreasonable.

It concluded that:

> Any other policy would result in confusion

detrimental to the purposes and efficiency
of our public school system.[21]

Two years later a sixteen-year-old Ohio boy
married a girl who was pregnant. The boy was not
only outstanding in basketball but also an excellent
student who was very popular with his classmates
and teachers alike.[22] The school officials had
established a marriage policy after civic and
community groups had requested it due to a "moral
problem existing in the community."

The Ohio Court relied on *Kissick* to answer the
athlete's charge of arbitrary and unreasonable
policy. It added several different arguments to the
previous ones in *Kissick*. The Ohio Court noted that
an outstanding athlete often receives too much
praise from his peers and people in the community.
It observed that fellow students try to emulate every
act of a "star athlete" from his speech to the type of
food he prefers, songs, etc.

The Ohio Court then answered the claim made in
most cases of this type that the athlete will lose the
opportunity for a college grant by not competing in
athletics. It said that an injury which is always
possible could in like manner eliminate his
opportunity just as well.

It then cautioned future boards of education to do
what is best for all students without considering the
pressure from adults who want winning teams and
large gate receipts.

In Louisiana a football player added a different
contention to the previous cases.

Allen Estay charged that the school rule prohibiting him from playing football was discriminatory because it denied him the same opportunities that unmarried students had.[23]

The Louisiana Court once again used *Kissick* as its guide and answered the athlete's contention by agreeing that all students should have the opportunity to attend school and receive the same treatment. It disagreed on the subject of extracurricular activities, however, by emphatically saying:

> Engaging in them is a privilege which may be claimed only in accordance with the standards set up for participation. It is conceded, as plaintiff insists, that he has a constitutional right both to attend school and to get married. But he has no "right" to compel the Board of Education to exercise its discretion to his personal advantage so he can participate in the named activities.

With such a background of judicial support for school boards' rules against married athletes' participation, it is interesting to follow the latest trend of the courts toward marriage and eligibility.

In Indiana in 1971, the Valparaiso School and the Indiana High School Athletic Association's rule on marriage was challenged.[24] The rule simply stated that:

> married students, or students who have ever been married are ineligible to participate.

The plaintiff, a high school football player

challenged the rule as a violation of his right to equal protection guaranteed by the Fourteenth Amendment.

While the Indiana Court did not feel that Wellsand's participation in football was "a Constitutional right," it did feel that he had the right of equal protection under the Fourteenth Amendment. The mere fact that athletic participation was not of "constitutional stature" cannot keep the individual from his rights, it observed.

In a dramatic change of attitude, the Indiana Court ruled that Wellsand would suffer more from the rule than the school would. In an approach that may reverse future policy, the court continued in support of the plaintiff by surmising that:

> in this case, the testimony is uncontradicted that the athlete is an exceptionally fine athlete who has an excellent chance of receiving such financial aid and will be greatly jeopardized if he is not allowed to compete during his final year of high school.

It then answered the question of judicial support for school authorities who try to operate a school with policies they consider beneficial to the students. The Indiana Court deviated from past concern for the school board by stating:

> On the other hand, no evidence has been presented by the defendants which would support a conclusion that any inconvenience or damage will be suffered by the

defendants if preliminary relief is granted
the plaintiff.

Accordingly, the court in Indiana reversed the trend
so apparent in previous cases, by granting Wellsand
an injunction to play football.

In Montana, Steve Moran, a seventeen-year-old
married athlete, was prohibited from playing
football.[25] By not being allowed to play, Moran
argued that his civil rights were violated. The School
Board based its defense on *Kissick* and other
previous cases that upheld school officials. It added
one different point when it vehemently stated that
the "presence of married students in
extra-curricular activities would result in reasonable
likelihood of moral pollution."

The Montana Court listened to the testimony at
the trial and then ruled that a meaningful education
must include the training of the body. It concluded
that "the right to attend school included the right to
participate in extra-curricular activities." This
attitude by the court represents a new judicial
concept toward education and athletics.

Finally, the court made several statements that
reveal the changing opinion toward high school
marriages and athletic participation. It established
the following points of view:

(1) To punish married students in order to
    discourage marriages among teenagers
    is contrary to public policy as above set
    forth.
(2) The married student has entered the
    most sacred institution in society, one

which society has chosen to encourage and preserve, not punish.

(3) It may be that teen-age marriages are to be discouraged but this cannot be done by discriminating against those already married without a showing of an overriding social interest.

(4) Steve Moran will be unable to play football in his last year of high school. The opportunities and benefits afforded by participation in this extra-curricular activity will be forever lost.

(5) The hardship resulting from granting the injunction will be much less and in fact may be negligible.

In granting Steve Moran the injunction to play football, the court concluded that it could not find any "moral pollution" or disruption of the educative process at the high school if he played.

It appears that the court has begun to make a definite transition from past decisions in behalf of defendant schools using *Kissick* as the model. It seems that *Wellsand* and *Moran* may become the controlling cases in such situations from here on.

IN MY OPINION

It has been said that coaches are conformists who are afraid of change. For several years my son's hair style has been longer than usual, but still in good taste. When I teased him about it, he quickly replied that for once in his life he could have hair and it really felt good. He reminded me that as a coach's son he was directed by his father to keep it short and neat. Yes, the same father who tried to teach him to think for himself, make important decisions, and not be willing to conform to the crowd. He was told to "be a man, and be willing to swim upstream against the tide instead of drifting downstream with the current." *But keep a crew cut by all means!*

Yet, it was interesting and revealing to watch him as a college graduate go for his first series of interviews for a teaching and coaching job. He did not cut his hair when he was interviewed in the urban centers of North Carolina, but before he went to conservative Eastern North Carolina off came the excess hair. He knew the stigma associated with appearance by some coaches and principals. He wanted a job, so he cut his hair.

Supreme Court Justice Hugo Black was right when he lashed out against students and parents who flood the federal courts with hair style cases. His admonishment to leave these cases to the local authorities made sense.

But does it? A principal read in the newspaper one morning that a court upheld a hair case for a defendant school and, buoyed by the decision, made an on-the-spot rule that all males would cut their hair to a specific length, determined by him, or face immediate suspension.

Arbitrary and capricious judgment and unreasonable action by many schoolmen open Black's recommendation to question.

Public opinion was strong over the story of Sylvester Hodges who elected not to wrestle in the

NCAA Championship because he refused to shave off his moustache. Hodges had worked tirelessly to get to the NCAA Championship but felt the rule, which had been ignored during the season, was unfair.

Many coaches seemed upset with the rule but when the NCAA polled 510 wrestling coaches, 490 favored the retention.

The Court has been inconsistent in ruling on hair style cases but consistent on its reasoning. Rules must be reasonable and essential to health, safety, team discipline and morale to be supported by the court. The Commissioner of Education in New Jersey may have set the guideline for all future hair cases in a 1970 decision.[26] The Commissioner made it clear that:

> Coaches may make rules that set the framework in which athletes must cooperate for the purpose of teamwork and organization. Such rules should be procedural in design and limited to practice sessions, training rules, and uniform requirements. Athletic coaches have the authority and duty to select team members based on individual competence. The opportunity to try out for a team activity should be based on talent and potential contribution to the team. The *reasonable* limits of any rules of eligibility should not include regulations on hair style and length, which are matters of personal taste, unless it can be shown that such styles create classroom disorder, present a clear and present danger to the student or his

fellow participants or are detrimental to
good health and hygiene.

On training rules, the court appears to be ruling
that school officials have authority to decide on
codes and subsequent penalties for their violation
but due process needs to be followed. It suggests
written rules that are publicized with proper
procedure for a hearing for offenders before action is
taken.

A new and possibly a definite trend seems to be
developing among the courts in its attitude toward
married athletes of both sexes. For years the court
referred to *Kissick* as its model for judicial
precedent in upholding school board regulations
denying married athletes participation in
extracurricular activities.

Now the court is quoting *Wellsand* and *Moran* and
ruling that the hardship imposed on an athlete by
prohibition of participation is greater than that of
the school. The court also insists that all students,
married and unmarried alike, receive the same
treatment regarding participation in both the
curricular and extracurricular.

The area of good conduct codes has always been
and will continue to be a controversial one.
Gradually, however, the reasons for adopting certain
rules will be changed by judicial fiat. In perhaps no
other area of athletics will the court attempt to give
the authority to regulate policy back to the schools
as in this sensitive area, but in doing so will demand
that reason be incorporated into the rules.

1. O'Connor v. Board of Educ., 316 N.Y.S.2d 799 (1970).
2. NOLPE NOTES, National Organization of Legal Problems of Education, Vol. 6, No. 7a, July, 1971.
3. Myers v. Arcata School Dist., 269 A.C.A. (No. 4) 633 (Tex. 1969).
4. Brownlee v. Bradley County, Tenn. Bd. of Educ., 311 F. Supp. 1360 (E.D. Tenn. 1970).
5. Gfell v. Rickelman, 313 F. Supp. 364 (N.D. Ohio 1970).
6. Neuhaus v. Torrey, 310 F. Supp. 192 (N.D. Cal. 1970).
7. Dunham v. Pulsifer, 312 F. Supp. 411 (D. Vt. 1970).
8. *Id.*
9. Griffin v. Tatum, 300 F. Supp. 60 (N.D. Ala. 1969).
10. *Id.*
11. Richards v. Thurston, 304 F. Supp. 449 (Mass. 1969).
12. Goldstein, THE SCOPE AND SOURCE OF SCHOOL BOARD.
13. Long v. Zopp, 476 F.2d 180 (4th Cir. 1973).
14. Massie v. Henry, 455 F.2d 779 (4th Cir. 1972).
15. O'Connor v. Board of Educ., *supra* note 1.
16. NOLPE NOTES, National Organization of Legal Problems of Education, Vol. 7, No. 4, April 1972.
17. Haason v. Boothby, 318 F. Supp. 1184 (D. Mass. 1970).
18. Van Alstyne, *The Students as University Residents*, 45 DENVER L.J. 582 (1968).
19. Stevenson v. Wheeler County Bd. of Educ., 306 F. Supp. 97 (S.D. Ga. 1969).
20. Kissick v. Garland Independent School Dist., 330 S.W.2d 708 (Tex. 1959).
21. *Id.*
22. State v. Stevenson, 189 N.E.2d 181 (Ohio 1962).
23. Estay v. Lafourche Parish School Bd., 230 So. 2d 443 (La. 1969).
24. Wellsand v. Valparaiso Community School Corp., Case No. 71 H 122 (2) (U.S.D.C. Ind. 1971).
25. Moran v. School Dist. No. 7 of Yellowstone County, 350 F. Supp. 1180 (D. Mont. 1972).
26. Harriss v. Teaneck Bd. of Educ., Decision of New Jersey Commissioner of Education (1970).

4. The 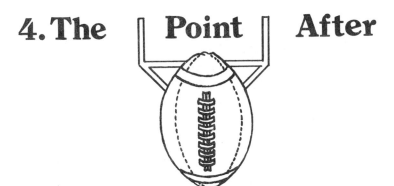 Point After

All 75 occupants, including 71 passengers and four crewmen, were fatally injured. The aircraft was destroyed.[1]

On October 2, 1970 near Silver Plume, Colorado, 14 players on the University of Wichita State football team, along with 16 other passengers, died when their charter plane crashed into Mt. Trelease.[2]

About one month later, on November 14, 1970, 75 occupants of a Southern Airways DC-9 carrying the Marshall University football team and boosters were killed when their chartered plane crashed at Huntington, West Virginia.[3]

The nation reacted with shock, horror, and total disbelief as 115 people were lost in such a short period of a month.

The Federal Aviation Agency immediately flooded the desks of athletic directors, following the two air calamities with safety information. In like manner, the state of North Carolina inspected every school bus route in the 100 counties, after a bus load of young children were violently killed on an unsafe, vine-covered bridge.

It is unfortunate, but true, that it takes shocking tragedies like these to get the *point* across and make people aware of the dangers involved in athletic travel. Today's athletes travel more than ever before, but little is done, in too many instances, to safeguard their lives with protective regulations. We are aware that our athletes, from little league to graduate school, travel constantly in every possible manner and on every type of conveyance available. While we realize that each method of transportation has its own unique problems, why must we wait until a tragedy takes place before we try to implement safe travel guidelines and procedures?

Too often it takes events that shock us to produce changes that should have been in effect prior to accidents. The administrator is beginning to recognize that travel is one of his most serious problems, and with litigation in the forefront, will hopefully create safe travel policies.

It is essential that administrators examine the various modes of travel with legal implications before setting policy.

Chartered Vehicles

The ideal way to travel may be the chartering of a commercial vehicle. Some schools will not compete interscholastically or intercollegiately unless they can travel by commercial carriers.

In New Jersey a school district chartered a bus to transport its pupils.[4] The bus left the road and hit a tree causing a fifteen-year-old boy to suffer crippling injuries. The school district refused to pay damages for the injuries and the parents sued the school district for payment. The court ruled that the school district had hired a bus company that had the proper insurance coverage required by the state. The bus company, in turn, had employed a well-trained, experienced driver. As a result of the accident, and the facts presented in court, the insurance company, representing the bus company, compensated the boy. In denying the parents of the injured boy relief from the school district, the court concluded that:

> A driver of a bus employed by one under contract with a board of education to transport school children is not entitled to be indemnified by the school board for liability incurred in that employment.[5]

Consider this when you realize that a school district in the same state was ordered to pay $1,216,000 for an injury in a physical education class due to an alleged lack of adequate supervision.[6]

A group of booster fans were traveling to a high school basketball tournament in Wisconsin when the bus struck the automobile of a faculty member who was driving to the game with his family.[7] The man was killed in the collision and his wife sued the school district for damages, alleging that the bus driver was negligent.

Once again the court favored the school district and supported its decision by emphatically pointing out that the:

> Legislature did intend that a school can delegate to others its tort responsibility or liability by contract.

The Wisconsin statute stated that a school district could provide transportation for extra-curricular activities but it was not mandatory.

These two cases give the administrator and coach reasonable assurance that chartered buses can offer a school or school district protection against damage suits when accidents occur.

Air Charters

Athletic teams rarely use buses, cars or trains today if trips are over 300 miles. Air travel has enabled teams to play games miles away and return the same day. Fewer classes are missed because of the time saved in air travel.

The Wichita State University and Marshall University tragedies in which entire teams were practically wiped out served notice on all administrators, responsible for travel schedules, to consider the dangers involved in such travel.

The Wichita State football team was traveling in two Martin 404's on the way to a game at Logan, Utah. The aircraft stopped at Denver, Colorado to refuel for the final leg of the trip. One of the flight officers deviated from the original flight plan so the passengers in his aircraft could take a "scenic route" and see ski resorts and other points of interest.[8]

The ill-fated plane crashed into a Colorado mountain, and a subsequent report, following a complete investigation, revealed that the accident was caused by the:

intentional operation of the aircraft over a

mountain-valley route at an altitude from
which the aircraft could neither climb over
the obstructing terrain ahead, nor execute a
successful course of reversal. Significant
factors were the overloaded conditions of
the aircraft, the virtual absence of flight
planning for the chosen route of flight from
Denver to Logan, a lack of understanding
on the part of the crew of the performance
capabilities and limitations of the aircraft,
and the lack of operational management to
monitor and appropriately control the
actions of the flight crew.[9]

In the investigation of the Marshall University
crash on November 14, 1970, the National
Transportation Safety Board reported that the cause
of the Southern Airways DC-9 crash at Tri-City
Airport in Huntington, West Virginia was due to a:

descent below Minimum Descent Altitude
during a nonprecision approach under
adverse operating conditions, without
visual contact with the runway
environment.[10]

Most experts in the field of aviation predict that
the number of aircraft will grow until they exceed
200,000 by 1979. According to the same forecasters
general aviation accidents will increase.[11] Since no
federal statutes exist in the area of aircraft liability,
and very few are recorded on the state level,
damages are usually determined by legal rules that
apply to accidents that take place "on the land or
water of the state where the accidents occurred." [12]
Legal liability varies with the different states, and

some states, for example, have guest statutes while others do not. In a state that has a guest statute, the plaintiff must prove that the operator of the vehicle involved was guilty of willful misconduct or its equivalent.[13]

The Federal Aviation Administration sent seventy-six colleges and universities in the Southwest a letter warning them of "fly by night" charters. The letter alerted all athletic officials to the danger that some charter companies presented them.

In a brochure entitled "Look Before You Lease" the Federal Aviation Administration stressed the fact, that while there are hundreds of legitimate aviation companies, capable of safe charter flights, there are also "dozens of other companies or individuals who have no legal operator's certificate for this purpose, and who are willing for the sake of profit, to risk the penalty of the law by evading safety requirements." [14]

The brochure cautions athletic administrators, who are lured by the inexpensive offers of certain companies under the disguise of a lease service, to take precautions in securing a charter. Sometimes operators may deliberately mislead a school as to who actually operates the aircraft.[15] Those who accept the "dry lease" will, in ignorance, find that they:

> are provided with an aircraft on a lease basis although it is actually serviced and flown by the leasing company. Such an arrangement (depending upon the terms of the lease) may make you the responsible operator of the aircraft, even though, in fact, you do not intend this and have nothing to do with the flight other than to indicate where and when you wish to fly.[16]

In the report on the Wichita State air tragedy, it was stated during the investigation that:

> none of the participants in this flight, the owner of the aircraft, lessee, or the company providing the crew and other services, acknowledged that they were the operator and accepted responsibility for the safety of the flight.[17]

The F.A.A. warns those in charge of scheduling air charters that while a charter company price might appear enticing because its fares are low, that very operator might not be certified and, in fact, cause you to break the law and put the lives of your personnel in jeopardy.[18]

> The F.A.A. recommends that any person or company providing and operating a large aircraft for compensation or hire must hold current F.A.A. certification as an air carrier, air taxi, or commercial operator. This certification is based on a showing by the operator that he satisfactorily meets the safety requirements of the Federal Aviation Regulations (FAR) Part 121.[19]

Finally, it is clear that athletic teams will continue to use air travel for contests that involve considerable distances. More and more air companies will seek the athletic business, and administrators will be faced with the question of which air charter company to use. The answer appears to be relatively simple if the F.A.A. recommendations are followed:

(1) Before you sign for a charter, ask to see the operator's F.A.A. certificate.
(2) If you are not certain of the status of the company, call the F.A.A. office in the local area for information.

Activity Buses and Vans

Many schools have purchased activity buses and special vans to transport students who engage in co-curricular activities. As in the case of aircraft liability, state statutes vary regarding activity buses that transport students in co-curricular activities.[20]

North Carolina has a law relating to activity buses or vans that differs from regular school buses. The local boards of education have the title for such buses even though a particular school has the use of the bus. Activity buses, unlike regular school buses, cannot be purchased with tax monies, but the transportation laws regulating inspection apply to activity buses as well as the regular state owned buses. The difference is that the:

> statute specifically provides that it does not constitute authorization for the use of state or local tax funds for the purchase, operation, or maintenance of activity buses.[21]

The cost and upkeep of such vehicles may be prohibitive to schools with limited financial resources. Although these vehicles are an improvement over the use of private cars, they often present problems that plague the administrators who are responsible for their use. In too many instances, the schools lack qualified drivers and delegate the job to a teacher or coach. Some states require the driver of an activity bus to "hold either a chauffeur's license or an operator's license and a training certificate from the department of motor vehicles." [22]

Many times the school activity bus or van is overlooked when inspection is needed and defects are present that present undue hazards to the occupants.

The University of Delaware was transporting its soccer team in two school-owned vans for a match

with Temple University in Philadelphia.[23] When
Gary Adams, a student who was driving one of the
cars, failed to stop at a traffic light an accident
occurred with the van driven by the coach, Larry
Kline. Although Adams failed to stop the car he was
driving and actually crashed into his coach's car, he
sued the University. He claimed during the trial that
the school officials were the guilty ones for several
reasons. He alleged negligence on their part in:

(1) Failing to determine whether the
plaintiff was a competent driver.

(2) Failing to instruct the plaintiff in the
correct operation of the vehicle.

(3) Failing to determine if the plaintiff had
a Delaware driver's license or a
chauffeur's license; and

(4) Failing to determine whether the
plaintiff met the requirement of
the Delaware statute to be 21 years
of age to drive a school bus.

Adams also claimed that the two vans were
overloaded and that this was the reason that the car
he was driving ran into the one driven by Kline.

The Delaware Court dismissed all the allegations
listed above with one exception. It considered the
argument that the van was overloaded to be a
question to be decided by the jury.

In New Hampshire, a case was litigated that
involved a vehicle that was used to transport
football players from the practice field to the
gymnasium.[24] Wallace Beardsell had finished

football practice and was trying to get on a truck that would take him to the gymnasium. As a rule, one of the coaches would supervise the loading of the truck and signal the driver with a whistle when it was safe to start the truck. On the day of the accident, the driver started the truck before Wallace was on it. The wheel of the truck ran over him causing serious injuries to him.

The school district argued that Wallace was guilty of negligence for failing to use reasonable care in the situation that existed. The court, however, did not support the contention of the school district but found it guilty, instead, of failing to supervise the truck properly.

Private Vehicles

A large number of school districts throughout the nation are forced to use private cars to transport athletes due to a lack of funds. Colleges and even many universities use private cars for the so-called "minor sports" because the high cost of commercial vehicles prohibits their use. With schools of all types adding leisure-time sports such as golf, tennis, swimming, etc., to their programs, and transportation costs rising each year, the problem becomes serious to school administrators. While private cars are not desirable because of the liability involved, their use will continue because of the expense involved in travel.

When automobile accidents take place, the operator of the vehicle is always held primarily liable for the negligent operation of the car.[25]

If the owner of the car is the one driving the car and the one directly responsible for the accident, the question of liability is clear. The owner and operator is liable if negligence is proved. In a large number of cases that come to court regarding the travel of students, the owner is not operating the vehicle. In such instances, the liability laws of the states differ regarding the responsibility for the accident. For this reason, school officials need to know the provisions of the statutes of the state in which they teach as they regard liability for transportation.

The majority of our states impose liability on the owner of the car under a rule referred to as the "Common Law Agency." This statute makes an owner responsible only when negligence has been proved of the driver who was under his employment or acted as his agent.[26] In most states, the owner of a vehicle is not responsible for the damages of a guest in his vehicle unless the driver was found to be grossly negligent.[27]

An unusual case happened in Arkansas in 1969, when a basketball coach used his private automobile to transport the members of his team to a tournament.[28] On the way home from the game, the coach was killed in a collision with another car. His widow sued for medical and death benefits from the insurance coverage the school had on the activity buses. The key point seemed to be that several activity buses were available at the time the coach **needed them but for some reason he decided to use** his own car. The activity buses did have adequate insurance for those who used them.

The widow's claim was rejected under the "Temporary Substitute Automobile" clause in the policy which provided coverage to vehicles that replaced the buses when they were out of use, due to repair or defective condition. Since none of the buses were out of service, the claim was denied.

Fellow teachers often let other teachers borrow their car when there is a need. While the spirit of cooperation is admirable, it may prove to be a costly gesture if accidents occur when another person is driving one's car.

An Idaho case in the 1930's is still a good example of what can happen if a borrowed car is involved in an accident.[29] The high school football coach borrowed the car of a teacher for a game that was to be played in a nearby town. The lady teacher was merely trying to be cooperative with a member of the staff, as many teachers are in similar situations. She did request that the coach drive her car instead of a student. On the trip the coach was killed in a collision and one of the passengers in the car was injured. The injured boy sued for damages.

The lady teacher who let her car be used became the defendant in the case as several issues were brought before the court. The issues raised were:

 (1) Was the injured boy guilty of contributory negligence?
 (2) Was the coach the agent for the teacher since he was driving the car?
 (3) Did the "guest statutes" apply in this case to the injured boy?
 (4) Was the coach guilty of negligence?

The court could not see how the defendant could claim that the injured boy was guilty of contributory negligence. When a coach or teacher in authority orders a boy or girl to ride in a certain car, team discipline usually demands that the person comply. As such, the court reasoned that he was not a guest and the guest statutes did not apply.

The court felt that the coach was the lady teacher's agent since she was promised that she would be reimbursed for the cost of the gasoline used on the trip. The court supported this decision by ruling "that agency is the relationship which results from the manifestation of consent by one person to another that the other shall act on his behalf and subject to his control, and consent by the other so as to act."

While the opinion of the court was not unanimous, the lady teacher was declared liable for damages.

A tennis teacher secured the services of a student to drive several girls home after practice each day.[30] The boy had the reputation of a "harum-scarum" type driver who had a car that was in defective condition. For every ten miles the boy traveled he was given one gallon of gasoline as compensation for transporting the students.

The boy was involved in an accident and the girls in the car were both seriously injured. The court found the school district guilty of negligence because it hired a driver with a bad reputation for driving and permitted the girls to ride in a car that had defective lights and brakes.

Guest Statutes

Rosemary Fessenden was a cheerleader at Heelan High School in Sioux City, Iowa.[31] The athletic director believed very strongly in the importance of cheerleaders for athletic contests. He required the cheerleaders to attend all home athletic contests and encouraged them to travel to as many away games as possible.

The athletic director gave a student permission to take a group of cheerleaders to a game in Sioux Falls, South Dakota. He did not plan to reimburse the student for taking the group and only cautioned him to be careful in driving to the game.

On the way to the game, the student who was driving the car lost control at an intersection and had an accident. At the time of the accident, he was driving between 55 and 60 miles an hour. Rosemary Fessenden sued the boy's father, who was the owner of the car, and also a passenger that night. She charged the driver of the car with "wanton and willful misconduct" and added that the driver was the school's agent. Rosemary thereby contended that the guest statute of Iowa did not apply to her situation.

The court ruled that the laws of South Dakota applied since the accident occurred in that state although all the occupants in the car were from Iowa. The South Dakota Code 1939 states:

> No person transported by the owner or operator of a motor vehicle as his guest without compensation for such transpor-

> tation shall have cause of action for
> damages against such owner or operator
> for injury, death or loss, in case of accident,
> unless such accident shall have been caused
> by the willful and wanton misconduct of
> the owner or operator of such motor
> vehicle.

The Supreme Court of Iowa upheld the decision of
the lower court in affirming the judgment for the
defendant. It ruled that the boy who drove the car
was not the agent for the high school nor was he
guilty of "willful or wanton misconduct." He was
simply guilty of "ordinary negligence."

James Truitt was a ten-year-old retarded child
who was injured in school in the state of Delaware.[32]
His teacher, Russell Gaines, took him home in his
car. Several days later the boy's mother called the
teacher and asked him to take her son to the doctor
since he was not improving and she did not have a
means of transportation.

On the way to the doctor, Gaines had an accident
in which James was injured. Mrs. Truitt sued the
teacher for damages. Gaines argued that the boy
was a "guest" in his car and not entitled to
compensation according to Delaware law.

The court disagreed with the defendant and
upheld the claim of the plaintiff. The court
interpreted the Delaware Guest Statute to imply
that a benefit did not necessarily mean money. In
this instance the district judge described the
teacher's act as

> rare in today's hardboiled world. But, it
> was the result of complex and

intermingling forces—obviously not for the purpose of pleasure and not alone out of a feeling to be helpful, for it did bestow upon the defendant a benefit in furtherance of his professional duties and responsibilities directed toward one of his retarded children. Under the statute, mother and son did not have guest status in defendant's motor vehicle within the meaning of the Delaware statute.

Judge Kalodner dissented and sympathized with the teacher's honorable intentions when he said:

The long and short of this case is that the defendant voluntarily helped one who needed help and asked for it. To say that doing the deed bestowed a benefit upon the defendant in furtherance of his professional duties merely emphasizes the intangible and speculative nature of the psychic reward a teacher may feel in altruistically helping a student and his family after school hours.

He concluded his dissent by strongly opposing the court's decision with these stinging words:

the derivation of this kind of "benefit" from a humanitarian act is not "payment" within the meaning of the Delaware statute.

Consider the multitude of athletic coaches who transport athletes under their supervision to doctors and even to their homes whenever transportation is lacking on the part of the school or parents. If Gaines is guilty of furthering his profession by the act of friendship, would the court possibly rule in favor of a coach who is interested in winning games? No matter what the reason might be for transporting athletes after school, or at any time, the coach would be suspect according to the *Truitt* decision.

One final case merits consideration as it relates to guest statutes. In the state of Illinois in 1968, a janitor asked the principal of the school if he could use several eighth grade boys to help him load a drag on a truck.[33] Five boys volunteered to help and this was all the principal thought they would do. On the way from the playground to the home of the road commissioner, where they were taking the drag, the truck was hit by a train at a crossing and all five boys and the janitor were killed.

Several of the parents sued the estate of the deceased janitor, the school district, and the Illinois Railroad Company. The issue was the status of the five boys who volunteered to help. During the trial it was pointed out that:

> a guest is one whom the operator of a motor vehicle invites to ride with him without financial or other compensation and where the relationship does not provide for tangible benefit for the driver.

The Illinois Guest Statute was quoted, in which it is clearly stated that:

> no person riding in or upon a motor vehicle or motorcycle as a guest without payment for such ride or while engaged in a joint

enterprise with the owner or driver of such
motor vehicles or motorcycle . . . shall have
a cause of action for damages against the
driver or operator of such motor vehicle.

The boys were not guests, claimed the plaintiffs,
since they were assisting the janitor, which was a
benefit to the school. The plaintiffs also contended
that the boys were not engaged in a "joint enterprise" with the janitor. To do so would mean that
they would be involved in some business in
which they would assume responsibility for the
operation of the vehicle. The court considered
these arguments and commented:

The basic rule of law is that if the
transportation confers only a benefit
incident to hospitality, companionship or
the like, a motor vehicle passenger is a
guest within the meaning of the Guest
Statute; but if the transportation is
primarily for some objective or purpose of
the operator, the passenger is not a
"guest" within the meaning of the statute.

The appellate court felt that the boys were doing
the school and its employee a service and that the
school owed them ordinary care. It agreed that
negligence existed in this instance but that it was
not willful or wanton misconduct. The court,
therefore, reversed the decision of the lower court in
favor of the defendants and remanded it for a new
trial against the school district and the estate of the
school janitor.

It upheld the earlier decision in favor of the

railroad since it did not find any evidence of negligence on its part.

School officials and coaches should take cognizance of this case before recruiting volunteers to travel in trucks or cars on school business.

IN MY OPINION

For some unknown reason, although school people are beginning to become aware and concerned over liability, transportation isn't usually included. We really do little to make safe travel policies or set up preventive action in the form of regulations, until tragedies occur.

Authors of administration textbooks urge all school officials to travel by commercial means. This sounds logical, particularly when you realize that the company you hire to transport your athletes becomes the one responsible for the payment of damages if accidents occur and you are sued. That is, if you are certain that the company you hire has the proper credentials and insurance coverage. How many of us in the position of authority, actually check on the company we use for hire? It is frightening and sobering to discover that some air charter company might fool you into using their services when you might be the one under the "dry lease" held responsible for damages in the event of an accident. Again, how many times have officials of athletic departments been contacted by companies offering bargain rates for travel, and yet these school officials failed to check on the credentials of the company?

It can be a simple thing to check with the various state departments of transportation or the Federal Aviation Administration, who stand ready to help you with the needed information, for just the price of a stamp or telephone call.

When schools can afford activity buses or vans, the danger of private cars with inexperienced drivers can be eliminated. These activity buses and vans do not solve all the problems of transportation, however, unless you set up periodical inspection, maintain safe buses, and provide well-trained drivers. Too often, we shift the responsibility of driving these vehicles to a coach, who, while an adult, may be responsible and interested in the safety of his athletes, but may lack the proper training to drive such a vehicle. School officials should check the statutes of their states regarding activity buses and vans since several states have statutes that vary from the laws regarding school buses.

When student drivers are used, safety policies should be established. School officials should be sure that the student meets the age requirement of the state, is competent and safe, has no traffic violations that are serious, and has a vehicle that is not overloaded or defective. A sample travel form that could be helpful to administrators can be found at the end of this chapter. It is good administrative technique to have each driver fill out the travel form and then keep it on file for the record.

Private vehicles, while a real problem to administrators, may become a necessity unless finances can be found for commercial travel. Let's be honest with ourselves and consider the typical situation that confronts most principals and athletic directors. A golf team has a match in a neighboring town during school hours. There are eight golfers on the team and one coach, not enough to charter a bus because of the expense for so few men. Two cars are needed for the trip. One car is driven by the coach but another adult cannot be located because of the time of day. Certainly, if safe travel policies are followed, the coach can select a student driver who can travel behind or in front of the coach's car. The situation can be successful as long as policies are adopted and enforced that stress safety.

When a coach passes up a van or activity bus that is available he should be aware of the consequences, if he is not covered by insurance due to a "temporary substitute automobile clause." The wise principal or athletic director will consult with the school attorney and insurance company and let the entire staff know their status. While this involves a moral responsibility, it is seldom practiced in reality.

Teachers should be very hesitant before they turn over their car keys to another person, whether he be a student or teacher.

Again, before lending your car, it is good to know just what status you will have if an accident occurs.

School officials should always use good judgment regarding the use of any vehicle. No defective vehicle should be used to transport athletes, no matter how short the distance may be. Use drivers with good reputations and, once again, use the travel form suggested at the end of this chapter.

Don't be too quick to rely on guest statutes as a defense if you reside in a state that has them on the books. Most coaches at one time or another take athletes home after practice when transportation is not available. Coaches do not, as a rule, hesitate to take injured students to the doctor or hospital in emergencies. The *Truitt* case in Delaware must make anyone pause and take notice. As the court said, your service may be "rare in today's hardboiled world" but it also may be interpreted as "a benefit in furtherance of (his or her) professional duties and responsibilities." [34]

Nor should a principal or coach who asks students to volunteer to help on an errand that involves travel feel that he can claim "guest statute" privileges if an accident happens. The court will not uphold such an argument or defense.

Transportation will continue to be a problem and administrators should set reasonable rules. The following suggestions should prove to be helpful in attempting to remedy the situation that faces those responsible for travel policies:

(1) Try to secure adult drivers when possible. If this is not possible, secure student drivers who have excellent safety records, and reputations for safe and careful driving.

(2) Use only cars that are in safe driving condition.

(3) Travel together whenever possible. Let the coach set the pace with safe speed.

(4) Don't overload the cars with too many passengers.

(5) Go as a team and return as a team. Avoid letting individuals return on their own unless their parents request this in person.

(6) If you drive passengers and receive expenses, take out a "rider" on your liability insurance to protect you.

Set up at least a brief form that can be used as a checklist before drivers are given the responsibility of transporting students:

(1) Check your policy so you know its complete meaning.

(2) Check serial numbers so you can see that they match the policy.

(3) Discuss accidents only with police or a representative of your insurance company.

(4) Consult your insurance company and go over your policy; it may be the wisest move you ever make.[35]

TRAVEL FORM

Sport _____

Coach _____ Adult Supervisor _____

Time of Departure (Date/Hour)   _____

Time of Arrival (Date/Hour) _____

Name of Driver _____

Is the driver also the owner of the car?_____ Yes _____ No

Age _____ Student ? Yes _____   No _____

Insurance Coverage: Type _____

Amount _____

Reimbursement of Driver: Gas _____ Oil _____ Mileage _____

Guests: Yes _____ No _____ (Status of occupants of the car)

Condition of the Car: Tires _____

Lights _____

Brakes _____

Wipers _____

Other Conditions _____
_____

License Number _____

Previous traffic violations _____

Signed _____
School Administrator

1. *Aircraft Accident Report,* National Transportation Safety Board, Washington, D. C., Report No. NTSB-AAR-72-11, April 14, 1972.
2. *Id.,* Report No. NTSB-AAR-71-4, Dec. 24, 1970.
3. *Aircraft Accident Report, supra,* note 1 at 3.
4. Hartmann v. Maplewood School Transp. Co., 254 A.2d 547 (N.J. 1969).
5. *Id.*
6. Miller v. Cloidt & Bd. of Educ. of the Borough of Chatham, No. L7241-62 (N.J. Super. 1964).
7. Lofy v. Joint School Dist. No. 2, City of Cumberland, 166 N.W.2d 809 (Wis. 1969).
8. *Aircraft Accident Report, supra* note 2 at 32.
9. *Id.*
10. *Aircraft Accident Report, supra* note 1 at 2.
11. AVIATION FORECASTS, Fiscal Years 1868-1977, Federal Aviation Agency.
12. G. I. WHITEHEAD, JR., THE LEGAL LIABILITY OF OWNERS AND OPERATORS OF GENERAL AVIATION AIRCRAFT, United States Insurance Group, at 2.
13. *Id.* at 3.
14. *Look Before You Lease,* Department of Transportation, Office of Public Affairs, Federal Aviation Administration, Washington, D.C., June, 1971.
15. *Id.*
16. *Id.*
17. *Aircraft Accident Report, supra* note 2 at 32.
18. *Id.*
19. Letter from the Department of Transportation, Federal Aviation Administration, Washington, D.C., June 30, 1973.
20. ALAN W. MARKHAM, PUPIL TRANSPORTATION IN NORTH CAROLINA, Institute of Government, The University of North Carolina at Chapel Hill, 1966, at 23.
21. *Id.* at 24.
22. *Id.*
23. Adams v. Kline, 239 A.2d 230 (Del. 1968).
24. Beardsell v. Tilton School, 200 A. 783 (N.H. 1938).

25. THEODORE MATTERN AND ANNE J. MATHES, DRIVERS MANUAL, New York Oceana Publishing Co. 1957, at 57.
26. *Id.*
27. *Id.* at 3.
28. Southern Farm Bureau Cas. Ins. Co. v. Noggle, 437 S.W.2d 215 (Ark. 1969).
29. Gorton v. Doty, 69 P.2d 136 (Idaho 1937).
30. Hanson v. Reedley Joint Union High School Dist., 111 P.2d 415 (Cal. 1941).
31. Fessenden v. Smith, 124 N.W.2d 554 (Iowa 1963).
32. Truitt v. Gaines, 318 F.2d 461 (3d Cir. 1963).
33. Enlow v. Illinois Central R.R., 243 N.E.2d 847 (Ill. 1968).
34. Truitt v. Gaines, *supra* note 32.
35. HERB APPENZELLER, FROM THE GYM TO THE JURY, The Michie Co., Charlottesville, Va., 1970.

5. The Double Standard

More and more, the female of the sporting species is demanding — and getting — equal treatment with the male.[1]

Women have created more change in sports than in any other area of athletics today. Women are demanding athletic scholarships, interscholastic and intercollegiate participation, in practically every sport, mixed competition in programs that have been exclusively reserved to men and, in general, all privileges that men have enjoyed for years.

Celeste Ulrich, commenting on the rise of girls athletics, insists that:

> The day is past when girls will have only the rationale of fairness as they require equal treatment. The law can now be invoked and in every case where the question of equality has been litigated, the women have won their case with ease.[2]

Ulrich describes the change in the status of girls athletics as a "whole new ballgame" and credits much of the improved role of girls athletics to litigation that is converting the attitudes and outdated social mores in society. Litigation is creating a face-lifting of sports for women and she cites court cases that involve:

> equal salary for coaching, equal use of facilities, equality of pay for both male and female officials, hiring policies with regard to potential pregnancy and equal opportunity to participate in coaching clinics and other activities restricted to only one sex.[3]

Bernice Sandler, director of the Association of American Colleges' Project on the Status and Education of Women supports this by stating:

> Women's use of the courts to resolve their grievances will be the second largest issue in the coming years because every institution in the country is vulnerable.[4]

"In addition to lawsuits already filed," estimates George LaNone, assistant to the director of the Equal Employment Opportunity Commission, "more than 500 job-bias complaints involving institutions of higher education have been filed with E.E.O.C. About 45 percent involve sex discrimination," he said.[5]

Ulrich's claim of increased participation for women in competitive sports is supported by several interesting cases that test the legal attitude of the courts.

In the summer of 1972, two women attempted to register for the all male North Carolina High School Coaching Clinic. When they were not allowed to register because of their sex, they vehemently argued that they were discriminated against, since, as coaches, they needed the clinic to improve their coaching technique and skill. Recently, the directors of the annual clinic announced that women can enroll for the first time in the history of the clinic.

In Florida, girls were denied the opportunity to participate with the boys in Little League baseball. California took an opposite view of the issue and permitted girls to compete on all teams sponsored by schools for boys. The California ruling prompted one critic to comment acidly:

> The California Chamber of Commerce must be correct; the sun in the Golden State is stronger than in Florida. It apparently fries the brain.[6]

The Upsilanti Orioles of Michigan defied an order by the national headquarters of Little League baseball and let 12-year-old Carolyn King compete and become the first girl to play in Little League baseball. In her first appearance as an outfielder she walked and was thrown out attempting to steal second base.[7] "Baseball is a contact sport," states Robert Stirrat, Little League baseball's publicity man. "It can be hazardous," he continues. "We have a five-page medical report which points out that girls are incapable of competing on the same level with boys. Their bones are more vulnerable, their reactions slower."

Dr. Stanford A. Lavine, an orthopedic surgeon in Washington, disagrees when he emphatically answers the charge by pointing out, "I can see no medical reason why a girl of 12, or younger, cannot compete in baseball with a boy of comparable age. If anything, girls mature much faster than boys because their growth line flows sooner." [8]

Mori Irving, a seventeen-year-old Piscataway High School girl, instituted a suit against the New Jersey Interscholastic Athletic Association so that she could play baseball on the high school team.[9] Irving was defended by the American Civil Liberties Union who supported her argument that she "had studied the fine points of catching by watching Cincinnati Reds star Johnny Bench." The New Jersey Interscholastic Athletic Association revised its rules in 1973 to allow girls to "compete with boys in bowling, fencing, tennis, track, cross-country, golf, swimming, and gymnastics but not in football, baseball, or wrestling." [10]

When a girl entered a basketball game that was played between two all male teams in California, the irritated opposing coach immediately took his team off the court and forfeited the game. In the same

state, a wrestling coach decided to see if he could use the same type of situation to his advantage. His 150 pound wrestler was injured and rather than forfeit the six points to his opponent, known for his "Swedish headlock", he put a 110 pound girl on the mat to replace the injured boy. When the boy quickly advanced toward the girl, the surprised coach removed her immediately from the mat before any contact was made.[11]

Even the time-honored practice of admitting women to sports events for one-half the regular price has been challenged. An angry male protested the Ladies Day custom and a racetrack in New York discontinued the practice.[12] Pressure from litigants caused the New York State Human Rights Commission to rule "that Ladies Day in sports arenas are illegal since they, in fact, discriminate against men."[13]

A group of students in Florida sued the NEA, AAHPER, and AIAW for preventing them from participating in athletic competition sponsored by the AIAW because they were recipients of athletic grants.[14] In reporting the case it was said:

> The main issue here is the right not to be treated differently. With respect to this suit, women are treated differently because scholarships are offered to men and not women . . . it appears likely that the school would be enjoined from enforcing the rules of the AIAW. A domino effect might be caused as other schools discover that they too are vulnerable and drop out of AIAW.[15]

The litigation is based on the 14th Amendment by way of the Civil Rights Act and the 1972 Education Act. Since the AIAW, is representing a state, it is considered to be a governmental agency and subject to a suit for discrimination.[16]

After the threat of the lawsuit, AIAW officials along with the approval of their member schools, voted to change the rules that were in effect.

The organization set new regulations for permitting financial aid to women athletes. The AIAW made it clear that it still had serious reservations regarding the new interim regulations when it reluctantly stated:

> We wish it to be understood that this practice (of awarding aid to women athletes) is not recommended but it is permitted.[17]

It then listed suggested regulations for schools to follow that granted women athletes scholarships. The recommendations included the granting of financial aid through the school committee, that is, the one that awards all regular financial aid; that grants be made for one year at a time, subject to renewal.

It set eligibility guidelines such as:

(1) An entering student must meet the institution's normal admission standards before being considered for financial aid.

(2) A returning student must have a minimum cumulative grade point

average of 2.0 (based on a 4.00 scale) at
that institution.

(3) To be eligible for renewal of financial
aid, a student must have earned 24
semester credits (or the equivalent)
between the beginning of one sport
season and the start of the same season
for next year.[18]

While it is apparent that AIAW does not approve
of the awarding of grants to women for athletic
prowess, some observers have claimed that the
giving of such grants:

points up to the dawn of a new era for
women on the collegiate, amateur and
professional levels.[19]

Still another predicted that:

Money is the big equalizer. Once they begin
to raise cash prizes, you can be sure that
women's lib has really arrived in sports.[20]

The Justice Department of Pennsylvania ordered
the State Department to disregard the regulation
that prohibited women from obtaining licenses to
wrestle and box. The court commented that after
watching women participate in a roller derby, no one
could possibly claim that women were the weaker
sex.

Women were thereby permitted to wrestle and
box against each other, but nothing was mentioned
about boxing or wrestling against men. The court
supported its decision by pointing out that according
to a 1971 amendment stressing equality of rights, it
could not limit licensing to men only.[21]

The New York State Board of Regents, in 1973, approved an amendment granting boys the opportunity to compete in sports that were open, formerly, to women only. If no boys archery team existed while a girls team did, boys could not go out for the team.[22]

The Board reaffirmed the 1971 amendment that:

> no pupil shall be excluded from such competition solely by reason of his or her sex.

The Regents stressed that this rule applies to schools in which separate competition is not provided for male and female students.

In 1972, anti-discrimination legislation was passed by the Board of Regents that clearly specified that no student could be denied participation in any academic or extracurricular course due to sex. The new amendment prohibits mixed competition in "baseball, basketball, field hockey, football, ice hockey, lacrosse, soccer, softball, speedball, team handball, power volleyball, and wrestling."

While separate competition is stressed in the sports listed above, the school's principal was given the authority to permit a girl to compete on a boys' team in "exceptional cases." [23]

A sampling of court cases will illustrate the attitude of the court toward girls athletics at various levels.

Johnell Haas qualified for the high school golf team but a rule of the Indiana State High School

Athletic Association prohibited her participation on the boys' team.[24] The rule stated:

> Boys and girls shall not be permitted to participate in interschool athletic games as mixed teams, nor shall the boys' teams and the girls' teams participate against each other in interschool athletic contests.

The trial court upheld the plaintiff's claim that the rule was unreasonable.

The Appellate Court recognized the voluntary status of the Indiana State High School Athletic Association but felt that it was a state agency and thereby subject to the equal protection clause of the Fourteenth Amendment. The Court noted that many high schools in the state of Indiana do not provide athletic programs for girls. The defendants listed several reasons for upholding the rule such as:

(1) Protection of girls' programs — if girls tried out for boys teams then boys would try out for the girls teams and possibly eliminate the girls program.
(2) The cost would be prohibitive if a girls program was instituted. For example, dressing facilities would be needed.
(3) Female supervisors for girls would be needed and the cost would rise for such personnel.

The higher court considered the testimony and concluded that the verdict of the trial court should be reversed. The court favored Johnell Haas because it reasoned that if athletics are beneficial to boys, why not to girls? It also stated that there was, in fact, discrimination since no program existed for girls while a program was provided for boys.

It stated that:

> Until girls' programs comparable to those established for boys exist, the rule cannot be justified on these grounds.

It admitted that separate dressing facilities would be needed but refuted the argument that female supervisors would be required when it pointed out that the IHSAA rules certify that all coaches be licensed and it did not matter who supervised the students of both sexes. The decision was close as three judges concurred while two dissented. One of the dissenting judges supported the Association's rule when he conceded that the thing that was at fault was the lack of a girls team in golf. He argued that the court was "making a 'back-handed' ruling to achieve a certain result. No demand has been made by the girls for a golf team and until they do the ruling should stand," he argued.

He then clearly stated his feeling about judges who act on school matters, when he cautioned his colleagues to remember that:

> We are judges, not school board members or athletic officials. We should avoid substituting our judgment for that of officials and parties possessing special knowledge of school conditions. We, as judges, should not sit on the school board.

A similar case originated in Nebraska where a girl was denied the opportunity to compete

interscholastically on the boys team by a ruling of
the Nebraska High School Activities Association.[25]
The decision of the court was summarized clearly
when it pointed out that:

> The issue is not whether Debbie Reed has a
> right to play golf; the issue is whether she
> can be treated differently from boys in an
> activity provided by the state. Her right is
> not the right to play golf. Her right is the
> right to be treated the same as boys unless
> there is a rational basis for her being
> treated differently.

Two girls got an Iowa Court to set aside two rules
that had been in effect for some time by the Iowa
Athletic Union.[26] One rule specified that girls had to
live at home with either their parents or guardians
to be eligible for athletic competition. The other rule
prohibited married women, mothers, or divorcees
from athletic competition. The Iowa Court supported
the girls by deciding that the rules of the Iowa
Athletic Union had violated the girls' rights to
privacy and personal freedom. The court also felt
that the rules were in conflict with the equal
protection clause of the Fourteenth Amendment
because:

> There is no such exclusion of male students
> who have the status of husband or father or
> both. The impact of such policies has been
> to discriminate against Jane Rubel on the
> basis of sex, males with the same statuses
> have not so been treated.

While the trend appears to be headed in the

direction of girls participation in mixed competition, especially when there are no comparable programs for the girls, many states still prohibit such competition.

Tracy and Lisa Kuehl, represented by their father, had met several times with the members of the school board in Pleasant Valley Community School District to seek equal treatment for female athletes.[27] When they were convinced that the Board did not plan to allocate funds on an equitable basis, they instituted a law suit asking $30,000 in damages.

The plaintiffs referred to a salary schedule in which the women coaches received lower salaries than the men. Testimony revealed that the Board spent 77.7 percent of the athletic budget for the males and only 22.2 percent for females. The plaintiffs claimed that the inequity of funds and the creation of "pep clubs and cheerleading squads" caused girls to be classified as second-class citizens and subjugated to males. The girls also contended that such treatment toward female students denied them the rights guaranteed by law under the Fourteenth Amendment.

Much has been said about the double standard applied by administrators in athletics to women but in *Kuehl* several unique arguments were presented. The plaintiffs listed the damages the alleged discrimination caused them, such as:

(1) They have been denied their right to try-out for and participate in interscholastic sports for which they are fully qualified;

(2) They have been deprived of the opportunity for development of their full athletic potential, thus limiting their ability to compete in amateur contests such as International Olympic Games and to compete and earn a living by participating in professional athletics;

(3) They have been deprived of the opportunity for full development of those qualities associated with athletic training and competition, such as self-discipline, confidence, sportsmanship and the will to excel;

(4) They have been placed at a disadvantage in competing for and obtaining athletic scholarships at colleges for which they would have been qualified had they been able to develop and demonstrate their proficiency in interscholastic events;

(5) They have been denied the opportunity to acquire the honors, awards, trips, publicity, and public acclaim associated with interscholastic sports;

(6) They have been humiliated and subjected to ridicule and mental stress and embarrassment by the continued refusal by defendants to recognize and encourage their desire to develop their athletic potential, and have been subjected to the status of second class citizens.

The case is pending as the plaintiffs are asking that the court enter an injunction against the school district prohibiting it from operating a program of interscholastic athletics until it can provide a program that is equal to both sexes.

Illinois, in 1972, refused to grant two female swimmers the opportunity to swim interscholastically with boys.

Two girls at Hinsdale High School wanted to swim on the boys interscholastic swimming team.[28] When they were not allowed to go out for the team, because of a state association rule, they sued the organization. The girls disputed a IHSAA regulation that prohibited competition between boys and girls in athletics. Once again the argument was that the rule of the State Athletic Association denies the plaintiffs the rights guaranteed them under the equal protection clause.

The court did not agree to the claim made by the girls. During the trial, testimony revealed that the girls wanted to compete on male teams until they had a separate team. It felt that if a program for girls was available the plaintiffs would not have sued the association.

The defendant athletic association disputed the girls' allegation. They argued in their behalf that:

    (1) The IHSAA and the Board of Education are not persons.
    (2) The challenged discrimination is not an action under color of state statute, ordinance, regulation, custom or usage.
    (3) The challenged discrimination does not constitute a deprivation of a right guaranteed by the Constitution and laws of the United States.

The court answered the defendants' three claims by reasoning that for "injunctive purposes" the athletic association can be treated as persons. It asserted that "all defendants may properly be enjoined as persons under 1983, but only the individual defendants can be liable for the damages sought."

The fact that state associations are composed of schools that are supported by public tax monies makes them responsible for the protection of a student's rights. 184327

The Illinois Court then commented that the classification of the swimming program by sex was rational. It then pointed out that the Olympic games, which represent the ultimate in athletic competition, the times of the men in sporting events are almost in every instance better than those of the women. The court noted that experts in athletics deplore the mixing of athletes and predict that if mixing is permitted "male domination of interscholastic sports" would result.

The court concluded that it would rule for the defendants in the instant case.

In Minnesota, two high school girls challenged a rule of the State High School Athletic Association. The rule denied girls the chance to compete in tennis, cross-country, track, and cross-country skiing.[29] The court in Minnesota, like the others across the country, concluded that the girls were not allowed because of their sex to participate on the boys team. It clarified its rationale in the decision when it said:

> The court is confronted with a situation where two high school girls wish to take part in certain interscholastic boys athletics; where it is shown that the girls could compete effectively on those teams and where there are not alternative competitive programs sponsored by their schools which could provide an equal opportunity for competition for these girls.

Cynthia Morris and another girl sued the Michigan High School Athletic Association for prohibiting them from participating in interscholastic tennis.[30] The Michigan High School Athletic Association had a rule that denied girls the opportunity of competing when one or both of the teams was composed of boys.

Cynthia Morris argued that the rule violated her right of equal protection as guaranteed by the Fourteenth Amendment. A district court judge agreed and issued an injunction against the Association's rule that prohibited athletes from competition on the basis of sex. The injunction seemed to apply to all athletic competition both in contact and noncontact sports.

The United States Court of Appeals considered the case and modified the judge's ruling. It clarified the ruling by adding the word "noncontact" to the rules of the Michigan Public Acts of 1972. The court agreed that girls should participate in noncontact sports but felt that contact sports were beyond the scope of its ruling.

The Division for Girls' and Women's Sports (DGWS) strongly opposes the new trends in athletics for women. Although they want all girls to have athletic experience if they desire it, they bitterly oppose mixed participation.

The DGWS spoke out sharply on this issue by warning that:

> The several court cases which sought to give girls the right to play on boys' teams could not be viewed as presenting a solution to the future of sports for girls and women. There are few girls who can qualify when competing with boys for positions on a team. This, then, means that the majority would not be served at all. Further, it is logical to postulate that in cases where girls have teams in sports that are unavailable to boys, the boys could request to play on the girls' teams. This would put us back where we started, with few, if any, sports opportunities for girls and women.

The DGWS believes that the solution lies in "separate but equal" facilities, coaches, equipment and funds, but not mixed competition. It argues that:

> while positive experiences for the exceptional girl or woman competitor may occur through participation in boys' or men's competitive groups, these instances are rare and should be judged acceptable

only as an interim procedure for use until
women's programs can be initiated.[31]

It is evident that considerable confusion exists
today regarding the role of girls in sports. Some
state organizations are permitting females to
compete in any sport with males, while others limit
competition to noncontact sports. Still other organizations keep the noncontact rule flexible and
give principals authority to use discretion in
deciding whether girls should play on male teams.

One thing is clear and that is that the future will
be one of court case after court case as individuals
test the laws that guarantee that institutions
receiving federal funds or tax money from public
sources will be required to share equally the funds
not only with the males but also the female athlete.

IN MY OPINION

A new day is dawning for girls athletics, and the
sooner this fact is recognized, the sooner law suits in
this area will cease. For years, girls athletics have
received the leftovers after varsity sports for men
with regard to finances, facilities, faculty salaries
and other practical items. The venerated arguments
that resemble "old wives tales" just aren't accepted
today. Very few educators believe any more that
girls are damaged psychologically, physically,
morally or emotionally by participation in sports.
The court has asked why athletics are so valuable to
males and not to females?

Bil Gilbert and Nancy Williamson in an article in

Sports Illustrated appear to answer the arguments of why girls athletics when they say:

> Women who have had the regular experience of performing before others, of learning to win and to lose, of cooperating in team efforts, will be far less fearful of running for office, better able to take public positions on issues in the face of public opposition. By working toward some balance in the realm of physical activity, we may indeed begin to achieve a more wholesome, democratic balance in all phases of our life.[32]

The court has considered suspect all facets of the athletic program for both male and female competitors. For example, the court will not tolerate a system in which the male can play in interscholastic athletics if married, divorced, or a parent if the same opportunity is denied a female with the same status.

Some associations have answered litigation by offering girls participation in any sport available to men. This may be fair but the questions of mismatching in sports like football with possible injury and subsequent lawsuits may drive dedicated but discouraged coaches from the teaching profession.

While the idea of mismatching disturbs many parents, coaches, and administrators others ask why this will be a problem. What difference is there in football, for instance, between a young 128 pound freshman halfback in tackling practice attempting to meet a 225 pound senior tackle head on as opposed to a muscular 175 pound girl doing the same thing? This is an intriguing thought but one that in all probability will not be answered until data is received on actual performances in the future.

It appears safe to say that schools will need to furnish programs in tennis, golf, track, volleyball, basketball, etc., to both sexes. If this is done, it is doubtful that litigation will be a serious problem.

It is obvious that agitation for equality in sports will dictate drastic changes. No one seems to agree on the direction we must go. It's a little like the man who was running down the street when a friend stopped him to ask where he was going in such a hurry. His answer seems appropriate to girls' athletics today when he says, "I don't know where I'm running to, but I don't want to be late." We may not know where we are heading but we know change must come even if it is wrong.

An example of hasty action that backfired came during the NCAA Convention in January, 1975. The NCAA Council proposed a pilot program under its direction that would set up championships for women in tennis and track in 1975 with nine others over a three year period. The Council felt that this would be an answer to the HEW's Title IX.[33]

The AIAW was meeting at the same time in Houston, Texas. The reaction of the women was immediate and violent.

One AIAW delegate summed up the reaction of the women when she said angrily, "In some circles, such forcible action by men toward women without consent is termed rape." [34]

The women made it clear that they have an organization for womens sports and don't want any male association such as the NCAA deciding how and when they will set up championships. The AIAW rejected the manner men recruit and stated that it felt they could develop a program of recruitment free from "excesses and abuses."

The question of financing dual programs will need tremendous appropriations in a day when a number of life-time sports are being added. Not only are sports being added, but financial crises are at an all time high. The courts may order equal budgets, facilities, staffs, salaries, equipment and other basic items but how will all these be financed by the schools? Sound thinking and planning rather than blanket rules are desperately needed if the problem of girls' athletics is to be solved.

1. ILENE BARTH, OUR WOMEN ATHLETES ACHIEVE NEW STATUS, PARADE, September 16, 1973, at 4.
2. CELESTE ULRICH, IT'S A WHOLE NEW BALLGAME, PROCEEDINGS OF THE FIRST NATIONAL CONFERENCE FOR SECONDARY PHYSICAL EDUCATION, Washington, D.C., 1972.
3. Id.
4. The Chronicle of Higher Education, Vol. Vii, No. 35, June, 1973.
5. Id.
6. The Review of the News, May 2, 1973, at 24.
7. The Star Ledger, May 12, 1973.
8. Greensboro Daily News, May 29, 1973.
9. The Star Ledger, April 11, 1973.
10. Id.
11. The Review of the News, February 28, 1973, at 23.

12. *The Review of the News*, April 18, 1973, at 23.
13. *Id.*
14. *Update, NEA and AAHPER Challenged in Courts on AIAW Scholarship Policy*, AAHPER, 1201 Sixteenth St., N.W., Washington, D.C., April, 1973.
15. *Id.*
16. *Id.*
17. JOPHER, GIRLS' AND WOMEN'S SPORTS, Washington, D.C., September, 1973, at 51.
18. *Id.*
19. PARADE, *supra* note 1.
20. *Id.*
21. Greensboro Daily News, June 12, 1973.
22. New York State Education Department News, Albany, New York, May, 1973.
23. *Id.*
24. Haas v. South Bend Community School Corp., 289 N.E.2d 495 (Ind. 1972).
25. Reed v. Nebraska School Activities Ass'n, 341 F. Supp. 258 (D. Neb. 1972).
26. Rubel v. Iowa Girls' High School Athletic Union, *Legal Aid Pact*, National Federation of High School Athletics, Chicago, Ill., Jan. 1972.
27. Kuehl v. Board of Educ. (U.S.D.C. Iowa), *Nolpe Notes*, Vol. 8, No. 12, Dec. 1973.
28. Bucha v. Illinois High School Athletic Ass'n, 351 F. Supp. 69 (N.D. Ill. 1972).
29. Brenden v. Independent School District 742, 342 F. Supp. 1224 (Minn. 1972).
30. Morris v. Michigan State Bd. of Educ., 472 F.2d 1207 (6th Cir. 1973).
31. PHYSICAL FITNESS RESEARCH DIGEST, President's Council on Physical Fitness and Sports, Washington, D.C., June, 1973.
32. BIL GILBERT AND NANCY WILLIAMSON, PROGRAMMED TO LOSE, Sports Illustrated, June 11, 1973.
33. Greensboro Daily News, January 9, 1975.
34. *Id.*

6. A New Game Plan

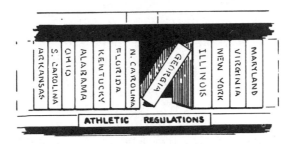

It remains a privilege founded upon the right to participate in what admittedly are activities forming an integral part of the school curriculum.[1]

For many years athletics were conducted on an informal basis, much as club sports are promoted in our colleges today. High school administrators refused to sanction athletics and would not assume responsibility for them.

When local rivalries developed and play became heated and often rough and rowdy, school administrators decided that some type of control was necessary to regulate play. Rules were devised on local levels to set guidelines that would promote equal competition.

The standards agreed upon often failed to achieve the goals set by educators as abuses continued in many schools. Various states as early as 1895 created organizations that would control athletics on the state level.[2]

Reece commented on the early state organizations when he said that:

> Controls were initiated by collective action of the schools as the need to eliminate abuse arose. Rules applying to the schools themselves and included in the By-Laws of the state association have had a similar history. The fact that many of the governing boards of the state associations, were and still are known as boards of control, provides rather conclusive proof of the philosophy that guided the early associations.[3]

For years the various state athletic associations have set policy regarding athletics and successfully implemented rules and regulations. Litigation has frequently been instituted against the associations but in almost every instance, the state association won the case. In the 1970-1971 National Federation Handbook, a statement illustrated the success it enjoyed in court. The Handbook boasted that:

> Each [case] has resulted in a decision that a State High School Athletic Association, in common with any reputable voluntary organization, has the right to enforce any reasonable regulation to which its members have subscribed as one of the conditions of membership.[4]

Today, the format or game plan has changed dramatically as the court is quickly changing its mood toward state athletic associations. The present day athlete is testing every regulation issued by state associations. The questioning of the validity and constitutionality of present rules may be caused by the diversity of regulations among the various associations.

For example, the Montana Association requests school officials to deny admission to athletic contests to any student who is unchaperoned.[5] The Washington Association declares an athlete ineligible if he accepts an award of over $35.00,[6] Alabama limits awards to $5.00 [7] while Oklahoma sets an even smaller limit.[8] A student who uses tobacco in Minnesota is suspended from athletics for three weeks for the first offense, with greater penalties for second and third violations.[9] Wisconsin forbids participation until a dentist attests to the dental fitness of the athlete [10] while West Virginia denies athletic participation to a student who is in the process of adoption.[11] All state associations have certain rules and regulations that tend to invite litigation against them. Some of the more litigated suits concern eligibility, good conduct codes, injury, dress codes, team membership, civil rights, all-star participation and girls' athletics.

Eligibility Cases in State Associations

The problem of athletes who transfer for various reasons has been a concern to all the state associations. School officials insist on rules that are intended to keep eager alumni and friends from enticing "star" athletes to transfer to their particular school. Rules regarding transfers usually create a hardship on legitimate student-athletes who pay the price for past violations and abuses. Three cases indicate the problem confronting the courts.

Andy Paschal transferred from Dan McCarty High School to John Carroll High School instead of Central High School in September, 1970.[12] In May, he was declared ineligible for the upcoming football season since the principal of Central High School refused to sign a transfer waiver for him. Since Andy was white, the Central principal explained that more white athletes would follow him and the result would soon be an all black school at Central. The court supported the Florida Athletic Association and made several noteworthy points when it said:

(1) There is no federal constitutional right of a public school student to play football; there is a federally enforceable right under the equal protection clause not to deny eligibility by state action, solely because of the player's skin.

(2) The privilege of participating in interscholastic athletics is outside the protection of due process.

A lower court in South Carolina restrained the high school league from denying two boys from playing football.[13]

Michael and Jerry Bruce transferred from a private school to the Blue Ridge Public High School although their residence did not change. The South Carolina High School League had a regulation that prevented transfers from playing for one year. It is quite clear that the rule was intended to prevent athletes from being enticed to change schools for various reasons.

The court concluded that the issue involved was the fact that the rule provided no exception, no matter why a person transferred.

The boys' attorney charged that the Association's rule was arbitrary and unfair since it denied the boys the right to participate in athletics which is a:

> fundamental segment of the educational process of our public schools and that their right to participate therein is commensurate with their right to participate in the regular classroom curriculum.

While the League officials agreed in part to the above statement, they argued, as do most officials of other associations:

> participation in high school interscholastic athletics is a mere privilege and not a right; and that the rule in question is "not arbitrary" and that the courts are without jurisdiction to enjoin its enforcement.

The League Officials claimed that Michael and Jerry Bruce did not have a right guaranteed by the Constitution to play sports. They strenuously defended their position, as do most other associations, by commenting that:

> Interscholastic athletics form a part of the extracurricular activities of the school and, as such, are protected under the discretionary powers of the various boards of schools. They are not a part of the

regular school curriculum and it is generally held that participation in such activities is a privilege which may be claimed by students only in accordance with the eligibility standards prescribed for participation.[14]

In essence the above statement sums up the issue before the courts today. On one hand, students challenge the regulations as arbitrary and the association defends the rules by alluding to the fact that athletics are not a right but a privilege subject to eligibility standards set down by a voluntary association. As such, it maintains it cannot be challenged.

The higher court listened to the arguments of the plaintiffs and the defendant and reasoned that the rules of the voluntary association applied to all students alike. It felt that the rule was adopted because past problems necessitated its adoption. All members agreed to abide by the League's rules when they joined and there was a provision that permitted students to play who were forced by court order to transfer.

Therefore, the higher court concluded that the lower court was in error and it reversed their decision and upheld the ruling of the South Carolina High School League.

Warren Sturrup attended high school in Miami, Florida during the 1970-71 school year. He moved to Bloomington, Indiana, during the summer of 1971 to live with his brother. Warren allegedly moved "because of the demoralizing and detrimental

conditions of his home and school environment."
Warren's brother became his legal guardian and he
enrolled in the local high school where he planned to
play football.[15]

Warren was notified in September that he was not
eligible for participation during the football season
because he was required under the Indiana High
School Athletic Association to put in a year of
residency to be eligible for athletic competition.

Warren claimed that he was eligible for athletic
competition because:

   (1) His move was necessary as a result of
       unavoidable circumstances; and
   (2) He established a new residence with a
       legally appointed guardian.

The trial court supported the IHSAA after citing
eleven cases in which courts ruled that state athletic
associations, being private and voluntary, were
worthy of its support unless conditions of "mistake,
fraud, collusion, arbitrariness or invasion of
personal or property rights" existed.

The plaintiff disputed the IHSAA rules and based
his arguments on a violation of his constitutional
rights. He claimed that the rule prohibited his
opportunity for an education. The court did not
agree with this argument since it did not feel that
the right to education included "interscholastic
sports and games."

Warren made a charge that obtained the favor of
the court when he asserted that the Indiana

Association's rule denied him the right to travel, guaranteed by the Constitution.

The court systematically considered the testimony before it made some timely observations:

(1) Sturrup was exercising a fundamental right in moving into this state. By withholding from Sturrup the privilege of participation in interscholastic athletics, the free exercise of this right was penalized. Therefore, the "compelling state interest" standard is controlling here.

(2) The record before us indicates that the one year residency requirement of the IHSAA is intended to serve two goals. One goal is to prevent the recruiting of student-athletes from one high school by other high schools. The second goal is to prevent school-jumping, that is, changing from school to school because of athletic rather than academic reasons.

(3) Schools are for education. There is no doubt that extra-curricular athletic competition may add to the educational process, but the extra-curricular activities should not take precedence over the curricular activities of the school. The sideshow may not consume the circus.

The Indiana Court then commented that it is a fundamental right for citizens "to move freely from state to state and from city to city within the state." It also felt the importance of the need to keep amateur athletics by rules but felt this was of a compelling nature, not a guaranteed right.

It therefore, with apparent reluctance, reversed the trial court's decision and chose to uphold the plaintiff by ruling that his rights to travel were violated.

Justice Sharp issued a blistering dissent on the majority opinion of the court in this case. In a long and detailed opinion he summed up his opposition to the decision by saying in part:

> I, for one, do not believe this court or any court possesses peculiar wisdom all of its own and can implement that wisdom by contriving and extending new constitutional principles and theories to impose that wisdom on the body politic.

He then reasoned that the case in itself was of little importance, except to Warren Sturrup of course, but that it:

> represents an open invitation to use the so-called right to travel to attack a wide variety of state legislative enactments and regulations. It is an invitation which I would not issue. It is an invitation in which I cannot join.

Until the courts settle the question of whether athletics are a right or privilege, countless cases of this nature will appear on the court docket.

Kenneth Williams played football for Booker T. Washington High School in Tulsa, Oklahoma.[16] Tulsa Washington, as it was referred to, had won all

four of its district games and was scheduled to play
Tulsa Hall in a State Four A Semi-Final game.

The principals of the Tulsa School District had
adopted a rule regarding eligibility that stated:

> A student may transfer from a school
> where his race is in the majority to a school
> where his race is in the minority and be
> eligible for athletics. A student who
> transfers from his home school to another
> school under the majority to minority (M to
> M) regulation is eligible to participate in
> athletics in only the school to which he has
> been transferred. *Should he return to his
> home school or transfer to another school,
> he must attend that school for two se-
> mesters to establish eligibility.* (Emphasis
> added.)

Someone reported to the Tulsa Washington
principal that Williams played football at Tulsa
Washington during the 1971 season, then moved to
the Tulsa McClain school under the M to M rule and
participated in track and tennis in the spring of
1972. In the fall of 1972 he returned to Tulsa
Washington and played football.

The Tulsa Washington principal immediately
reported the situation to the Oklahoma Secondary
School Activities Association. The Executive
Secretary of the Association enforced the
organization's rules and declared the player
ineligible and the school unable to compete for the
playoffs.

The Oklahoma Secondary School Activities
Association and the Executive Director were named

defendants in a law suit in which the plaintiffs tried
to get the court to prohibit the Oklahoma
Association from interfering with the playoff game.
The player and the Tulsa Washington school were
not the plaintiffs and did not institute the litigation.

The Supreme Court of Oklahoma reviewed the
facts in the case and ruled that it found "no evidence
of fraud or collusion, or that the defendants acted
unreasonably, arbitrarily, or capriciously." It
concluded that the Oklahoma Association should be
allowed to enforce its rules and regulations without
interference. It noted that neither the athlete
involved nor the school that was declared ineligible
had sought relief in the court and therefore favored
the defendant, Oklahoma Athletic Association.

Repeating Grades

Three students sued the athletic association in
Louisiana because they were denied participation in
athletics.[17] The three boys had passed the eighth
grade the previous year, but decided to take the
grade over. The boys claimed that they had not been
told that repeating a grade previously passed in
junior high school could make them ineligible for
athletics. They felt that their rights under the equal
protection clause of the 14th Amendment had been
violated. The court disagreed and felt the case did
not warrant federal action and thereby dismissed
the case.

John David of Covington, Louisiana was given
academic tests to see if he could enter a school in
New Orleans.[18] As a result he was turned down by

two New Orleans schools but accepted by a third on the condition that he repeat the eighth grade. Later he was declared ineligible since he repeated the grade. His father argued that the rule was retroactive because the school had not been a member of the Louisiana Athletic Association when his son transferred and that an exception should be made.

The court discounted his argument because it felt that the school agreed to accept all of the state association regulations at the time it joined. The decision was also supported by the appellate court which felt that the Louisiana Association was a voluntary organization and as such the court did not have the authority to interfere with its conduct of business as long as it was fair and honest in its rulings.

Rodney Saunders' team was outstanding in football and had won the right to advance to the state playoffs.[19] The Executive Committee of the State Association declared Rodney ineligible because he had not attended the high school for a full year. The Committee also forfeited all of the games in which he played, levied a fine and put the school on probation for one year.

The decision of the Committee was immediately challenged in court, but once again the court upheld the ruling on the basis that the association was voluntary and private and not subject to judicial interference.

Summer Camps and Clinics

Most states have summer camps in practically every interscholastic sport. In Minnesota, however, the athletic association opposed summer programs. James Brown, a 16-year-old hockey player, was upset because he was told that attendance at a hockey school, camp, or clinic, unless approved by the league's board of control, would cost him his eligibility.[20]

The league officials stressed the reasonableness of the rule by pointing out that it removed the pressure from adolescent athletes, so often put on them by peer groups and parents. They also argued that, since poorer students could not afford to attend such camps, this precluded a fair level of opportunity for all students. Finally, they stated that the rule helped avoid overemphasis in athletics that often develops when a program is taken out of the educational environment of the school.

The trial court heard the arguments of the league officials but favored the plaintiff by ruling that:

> Jim has a constitutionally protected right to participate in hockey competition at Roosevelt High School and to compete for team membership so long as he has violated no law and no rules.

It made an additional comment that reinforced the attitude of some courts in previous decisions when it emphasized:

> It remains a privilege founded upon the right to participate in what admittedly are

activities forming an integral part of the
school curriculum. In this case (plaintiff)
cannot properly be deprived of that right
and the possibility of qualifying for the
privilege by reason of a possible violation of
rules having no directly related school
purpose and not necessary to the school
welfare.

The Supreme Court of Minnesota reviewed the
validity of the lower court verdict but revised it,
because it felt that the court has always supported
regulations adopted by authorities who are
responsible for the administration of school
programs. The exception comes when the court finds
the rules to be unreasonable and arbitrary in nature.
In this case, the rules were judged to be fair and
reasonable.

A Missouri case mirrored the attitude of the
Minnesota court regarding summer camps.[21] The
plaintiff operated a baseball camp during the
summer for boys from nine to twenty-two years of
age. The owner of the camp stressed the fact that his
camp taught fundamental baseball in a manner that
was aimed to improve the basic skills of the boy. He
claimed that the program did not put any emphasis
on competition.

In 1970 the Missouri State High School Athletic
Association put into effect a rule that had been
recommended to it by the National Federation. The
rule provided the following restrictions regarding
summer camps:

(1) A secondary school student who attends
    a camp specializing in one sport for
    more than two weeks during the
    summer shall lose his eligibility the
    following year to represent his school
    in that particular sport;
(2) While schools can conduct their own
    camps for up to two weeks, a student is
    not permitted to participate in both a
    school camp for two weeks and a
    non-school camp for another two weeks
    when both camps specialize in the
    same sport.

The rule permitted boys to attend a camp that
offered a variety of sports and did not specialize in a
particular sport.

The baseball camp's enrollment was reduced in
1970 and the plaintiff attributed the loss to the rule

of the Missouri Athletic Association. The plaintiff refuted the arguments of the Missouri Athletic Association in which it advocated that specialized summer camps were detrimental to the athlete and the rule was necessary because it:

(1) helped prevent inequalities and unfair advantages with different economic means, as well as between schools located in areas of differing economic wealth;
(2) helped prevent conflicts between campers and their coaches over theory;
(3) was necessary to prevent young students from being "burned out" in a sport;
(4) promoted development of the whole child by preventing premature specialization and by exposing students to sports in which they could participate throughout life;
(5) helped prevent overprofessionalism, exploitation and undue pressure on students from parents, coaches, and booster clubs;
(6) the two-week period represented a balance between no camp at all and the alleged abuses of a prolonged camp.

The plaintiff disagreed with each point and countered by arguing that the Association did not have the right to dictate to parents or students what they could "do during a vacation period." It questioned the inconsistency of the two-week rule when co-curricular activities such as music were not covered by a similar rule.

The Missouri Court of Appeals reviewed the trial court's action in which it favored the defendant, Missouri Athletic Association. It then made several timely observations when it supported the Association's authority to make rules that are reasonable. It stated that:

> Along with entrusting the education of our children to teachers and administrators, we also entrust the control and supervision of the extra-curricular activities incident to that education.

It continued by explaining that:

> it is obvious that chaos would result without such rules. It is also obvious that the members are in the most advantageous position to appreciate the regulations under which they must act to achieve desired goals.

It then made a strong statement that clearly illustrated its attitude toward judicial interference in such matters as summer sport camps when it concluded that:

> A court should not interfere with the enactment of those regulations as long as they are reasonable and do not infringe on public policy or law.

The Court of Appeals then affirmed the trial court's ruling by agreeing that the rule was reasonable.

Good Conduct Code

A fascinating case came before the Supreme Court

of Iowa in 1971, and the decision in this case has
many interesting facets that could have a
far-reaching effect on the operation of state athletic
associations in the future.[22]

William Bunger and three minors were riding
together on June 7, 1971 when a policeman stopped
them and discovered a case of beer in their car.
Three of the boys pleaded guilty to the possession of
beer, but William Bunger pleaded not guilty and the
charge against him was dropped. William reported
the incident to the athletic director of his high school
three days later and admitted that he had been
aware of the presence of the beer in the car. By rules
of the Iowa High School Athletic Association he was
declared ineligible for six weeks beginning with the
start of the football season. He took the case to
court, but the lower court supported the rule of the
Iowa State Athletic Association. He then appealed
the decision to the Supreme Court of Iowa where the
Supreme Court Justices considered two issues to be
basic in the case:

(1) Does the Iowa High School Athletic
Association have authority to pro-
mulgate the rule in question?
(2) Is the rule valid on its merits?

The court examined the vast number of previous
cases and commented that:

Rule-making by school boards involves the
exercise of judgment and discretion. The
legislature has delegated rule-making to
those boards and the general principle is
that while a public board or body may

authorize performance of ministerial or
administrative functions by others it
cannot redelegate matters of judgment or
discretion.

The court insisted that the rules in this case were
not really local rules but rules set by the Iowa
Association; it added:

Again a school which joins the Iowa High
School Athletic Association after a number
of rules have been adopted has no choice as
to the rules that it will accept. It must take
them all and abdicate its non-delegable
responsibility to select the rules it wishes to
have. Then what about a member school
which becomes dissatisfied with a rule? It
has no power to repeal the rule. To say the
school can withdraw from IHSAA is no
answer. If it leaves IHSAA voluntarily or
involuntarily for violating the rules its boys
interscholastic program is at an end —
except for playing Kalona its hands are
tied. The power is actually in the
Association, not each school board where
the statute places it.

It then analyzed the situation as one in which an
organization started out as a vehicle to schedule
games and tournaments and continued to grow until
it regulated all matters that came under the heading
of athletics. On the merits of the beer rule itself, the
court compared the effect of misconduct at school
and at home and felt that the home was responsible
for behavior out of school. It did agree that
stand-out athletes, students or others engaging in
extra-curricular activities did have a special

responsibility for good conduct since many schools look up to them for leadership. It also agreed that an athlete could be penalized by school officials for drinking beer during the football season. It strongly argued however, that the rule in question was:

> too tenuous since it was beyond not only the football season but also the school year.

The court reasoned that the school officials were entering an area properly left to civil authorities and for this reason decided that the rule was not valid. The Court did not believe that the rule conformed to the test of reasonableness. In closing, the court once more defined its thinking on the case when it commented:

> This particular rule is not confined to the consumption of beer or even to the acquisition, disposition, possession or transportation of beer. It imposes ineligibility for mere occupation of a car containing beer with knowledge of the presence of the beer and when beer is discovered by an officer. School authorities may make reasonable beer rules, but we think this rule is too extreme. Some closer relationship between the student and the beer is required than mere knowledge that the beer is there. The rule as written would even prohibit a student from accepting a ride home in a car by an adult neighbor who had a visible package of beer among his purchases. We realize that the rule has been made broad in an effort to avoid problems of proving a connection between a student and the beer. But rules cannot be so

extended as to sweep in the innocent in order to achieve invariable conviction of the guilty.

The rule was reversed in favor of the plaintiff.

IN MY OPINION

For too many years, state high school athletic associations have promulgated rules and regulations intended to set guidelines and standards for schools to follow. High school coaches and principals have, in most cases, placidly accepted the rules of their associations without complaint or thoughts of challenge in the courts. The associations' rules were in many cases a means to an end, since individual schools and coaches could not enforce a rule that might be unpopular in a particular situation. Under the vast umbrella of the state association, however, regulations such as the "beer rule" in Iowa could reinforce and support the desires of a school or coach who otherwise could not enforce such a rule.

Today the whole picture has changed drastically and students and parents alike challenge any and all rules they feel are arbitrary or unreasonable. A Yale Law School graduate recently commented that the people in his school district were ultra-sophisticated when it came to law, and he caustically commented that, even with his education, the laymen put him to shame with their unbelieveable knowledge of law. In his particular school district, litigation against coaches, teachers and principals has risen at a fantastic rate.

State association officials do not welcome the litigation, but then who does? Perhaps the lawyer who hopes to represent a client on a contingency fee basis might actively seek and welcome lawsuits, but, generally, few people do. While trials are unpleasant for most people, few state associations are taking the time to review and update their regulations to meet the demands of a changing age. Ziegler in *Athletics in America*[23] decries the lack of change and the unwillingness to adjust when he blasts the coaching profession because:

> We are conformists who want to preserve the status quo at almost any cost. We are the educators anxious to keep order and discipline.

He continues realistically:

> We in all probability need a different ideal for today that is based upon a conception of man on earth moving into the twenty-first century.

A business as usual attitude causes us to live with antiquated, arbitrary and antagonistic rules that have become vulnerable to the changing mood of progressive courts. No longer will blind obedience suffice for the coach who boasts that his players will "literally run through a brick wall, if asked to do so."

At a meeting of a state athletic advisory board, I heard outstanding people get upset and dismayed over a lack of grooming on the part of some athletes in a few schools throughout the state. Several people at this meeting urged a uniform dress code, standards for grooming and hair length, and other so-called "necessary regulations." While their sentiments were shared by the majority present, wiser words were spoken that cautioned each school to handle its own situation on a local level.

Many of the suits in the court really do not belong there, in my opinion. We are litigating practically everything and anything, and it may not be too long before a justice speaks out vehemently against the trivia that is flooding the court dockets.

While the courts still favor the state high school athletic associations, there is no guarantee of immunity for any rule on the basis of voluntary membership. When a rule or regulation is considered to be *arbitrary* or *unreasonable* the bias ends.

State high school athletic associations are being challenged on eligibility cases in rising numbers. The court has made observations that are interesting to consider. It has stated that the privilege of interscholastic athletic competition is outside the protection of due process and that a student is not given a federally "constituted right" to participate in a sport unless his rights under the equal protection clause are violated.

The courts continue to debate the argument of privilege or right when athletics are involved and, when this basic and fundamental question is settled in the courts, the whole picture involving athletics will change remarkably.

At the present time, the courts believe that athletes should have the opportunity to attend private summer camps and clinics in any sport and not be denied this chance unless the individual violates a law. The court still considers such participation a privilege founded upon a right if the activities are a part of the total curriculum of the school. Many educators urge that all athletics be considered extra-curricular and therefore a privilege. They feel this will stop almost all litigation.

Still other state agencies, such as the New York Board of Regents, treats the extra-curricular program the same as the academic or curricular. These agencies do not consider athletics to be a privilege but feel that it is a right open to all individuals, regardless of race, creed, color, or sex.

Good conduct codes may be approved, but the court will tolerate fewer and fewer instances of innocent people being penalized in order to catch a guilty person.

Finally, a very important ruling has been made when a court looked long and hard at the function of a state association with its numerous rules and regulations.

When state associations take over the function of rule-making that has been delegated by the legislature to a school board, the move will be opposed by the court. The court made its position clear when it insisted that redelegation of rules that require judgment or discretion will not be tolerated by the court. Local school boards have the responsibility of using discretionary powers granted by the state to set rules. The court does not believe that athletic associations can take over this power. School boards will be in a vulnerable position when they redelegate this rule-making power to state associations.

It is true that once upon a time state high school athletic associations were not subject to adverse verdicts against them, but that day is over. If associations want to eliminate expensive litigation, they can do so by updating their rules and regulations in a manner that will fit the times in which we live and will be fair and reasonable. It is truly time that this takes place — it is a "whole new ball game."

1. Brown v. Wells, 181 N.W.2d 708 (Minn. 1970).
2. Milton Reece, Litigation Involving the Individual High School Athlete, 1973 (unpublished paper, University of North Carolina at Greensboro).
3. *Id.*
4. NATIONAL FEDERATION HANDBOOK, Chicago, Illinois, 1970-71.
5. MONTANA HIGH SCHOOL ASSOCIATION, 1971-72, at 56.
6. WASHINGTON INTERSCHOLASTIC ACTIVITIES ASSOCIATION HANDBOOK, 1971-72, at 37.
7. ALABAMA STATE ATHLETIC ASSOCIATION HANDBOOK, 1971, at 91.
8. OKLAHOMA SECONDARY SCHOOL ACTIVITIES ASSOCIATION HANDBOOK, 1971-72, at 28.
9. MINNESOTA STATE HIGH SCHOOL LEAGUE, 1971-72, at 23.

10. WISCONSIN INTERSCHOLASTIC ATHLETIC ASSOCIATION HAND-BOOK, 1971-72, at 28.
11. WEST VIRGINIA SECONDARY SCHOOL ACTIVITIES COMMISSION HANDBOOK, 1970, at 33.
12. Paschal v. Perdue, 320 F. Supp. 1274 (S.D. Fla. 1970).
13. Bruce v. South Carolina High School Athletic Ass'n, Opinion No. 19441, June, 1972.
14. *Id.*
15. Sturrup v. Mahan, 290 N.E.2d 64 (Ind. 1972).
16. Oklahoma Secondary School Activities Ass'n v. Midget, 505 P.2d 175 (Okla. 1972).
17. Mitchell v. Louisiana High School Athletic Ass'n, 430 F.2d 1155 (5th Cir. 1970).
18. David v. Louisiana High School Athletic Ass'n, 244 So. 2d 292 (La. App. 1971).
19. Saunders v. Louisiana High School Athletic Ass'n, 242 So. 2d 19 (La. App. 1970).
20. Brown v. Wells, 181 N.W.2d 708 (Minn. 1971).
21. Art Gaines Baseball Camp v. Houston, No. 34693 (Mo. Ct. App., Oct. 9, 1973).
22. Bunger v. Iowa High School Athletic Ass'n, 197 N.W.2d 555 (1972).
23. EARLE F. ZIEGLER, ATHLETICS IN AMERICA, Oregon State University Press, Corvallis, Oregon, 1972.

7. It's A Whole New Ball Game

We cannot rely on the benevolence of the schools or coaches, we must protect the health and safety of our athletes with federal legislation.

Hon. Ronald V. Dellums
of California

The University of Oklahoma, winner of the Big Eight Championship in football in 1972, was penalized by the NCAA for recruiting irregularities. As a result the University of Oklahoma was forced to forfeit its regular season wins, its Big Eight title and serve two years probation. The school was also denied the opportunity of appearing on national television during the probationary period.[1]

Southwestern Louisiana University's highly successful basketball program received the "most severe penalty in NCAA history" when it was compelled to drop basketball for two years and face the possibility of expulsion from the NCAA.[2]

The NCAA cited over 100 charges against the

school. Some of the complaints were that the
University:

> provided expensive wardrobes for athletes;
> free transportation for players' parents,
> and girl friends; payment of automobile
> traffic tickets, rents, and bills; funding a
> honeymoon trip for a prospective athlete;
> forgery of high school documents; and
> furnishing substitute scholars for college
> tests.[3]

Most schools are governed by some regulatory
body that sets policy and enforces regulations
regarding standards for competition. Some of the
organizations are the National Collegiate Athletic
Association (NCAA), the National Association of
Intercollegiate Athletics (NAIA), The Athletic
Intercollegiate Association for Women (AIAW), the
Division of Girls' and Women's Sports (DGWS) and
the Amateur Athletic Union (AAU).

During the past few years, these organizations
have implemented rules designed to control athletics
on a sane and equitable basis. With the advent of
controls and regulations new litigation has
developed in many areas and against various
associations and regulatory bodies.

Several cases are typical of recent litigation that
has come before the courts.

Gregg Taylor signed a grant-in-aid form to play
football at Wake Forest University in 1967.[4] The
form which was adopted for use by the Atlantic
Coast Conference stated:

> This grant, if awarded, will be for four
> years provided I conduct myself in

accordance with the rules of the
Conference, the NCAA and the Institution.
I agree to maintain eligibility for
intercollegiate athletics under both
Conference and Institutional rules.
Training rules for intercollegiate athletics
are considered rules of the Institution, and
I agree to abide by them.

The form then covered the athlete's status in the
event he was injured by providing that:

If injured while participating in athletics
supervised by a member of the coaching
staff the Grant or Scholarship will be
honored; the medical expenses will be paid
by the Athletic Department . . . .

It concluded by stating:

that this grant, when approved, is awarded
for academic and athletic achievement and
is not to be interpreted as employment in
any manner whatsoever.

The NCAA has for many years been attempting to
protect student-athletes from unfair practices by
coaches. In the past, athletes have been dropped
from athletic grants when coaches felt they lacked
the ability to win games for them. In some
instances, athletes have charged that coaches made
life so miserable for them that it was easier to quit
and give up their grants than to stay out for the
various teams.

With these abuses in mind, the NCAA had the
following rules in effect when Taylor signed the

Atlantic Coast Conference Application, that prohibited:

(a) Graduation or cancellation of institutional aid during the period of its award on the basis of a student-athlete's prowess or his contribution to a team's success.

(b) Graduation or cancellation of institutional aid during the period of its award because of any injury which prevents the recipient from participating in athletics.

(c) Graduation or cancellation of institutional aid during the period of its award for any other athletic reason, except that such recipient (1) voluntarily renders himself ineligible for intercollegiate athletic competition, or, (2) fraudulently misrepresents any information on his application, letter of intent or tender, or engages in serious misconduct warranting substantial disciplinary penalty.

The NCAA then added another safeguard into its regulations by stipulating that athletic recipients could have their scholarships reduced or cancelled only when:

(1) such action is taken by the regular disciplinary and/or scholarship awards authorities of the institution.

(2) the student has had an opportunity for a hearing, and

(3) the action is based on institutional policy applicable to the general student body.

Wake Forest University did not have a policy on grants-in-aid at the time Gregg Taylor signed such a Conference application. According to testimony during the trial, the policy was adopted several years later. A statement was included in the athletic department's policy that required attendance at practice to keep a grant-in-aid. Dr. Gene Hooks, the Athletic Director, pointed out that such a regulation was in fact part of athletic policy for the thirty years the school granted athletic scholarships.

A review of the facts in the case revealed the following information. Gregg Taylor entered Wake Forest in 1967 and played football that fall. After the first semester, his academic average fell below the standard required by Wake Forest. The institution required an average of:

    (1) 1.35 freshman year
    (2) 1.65 sophomore year
    (3) 1.85 junior year

Gregg decided to forego spring practice so he could build his 1.0 average (based on a 4.0 scale) up to acceptable standards. He notified his football coach of his plans and succeeded in attaining a 1.9 average which was well beyond the required freshman average.

Gregg then decided not to play football in the fall and achieved a 2.4 grade average. He did not report for spring practice his sophomore year either. Gregg received notification from school officials that the Faculty Athletic Committee would consider his situation since he refused to participate in the football program for which he had been awarded a scholarship. The Athletic Committee recommended that his grant be ended and the scholarship committee approved the action. At the end of his sophomore year, Gregg's grant was terminated.

Gregg returned to Wake Forest for his junior and senior years and graduated in 1971. He and his father instituted a suit against Wake Forest University to recover $5500 which they claimed was the cost of his final two years. The plaintiffs based their claim on the fact that participation in football hindered Gregg's academic progress and argued that he acted "in good faith in refusing to participate in the football program."

The North Carolina Court of Appeals supported the action taken by the University. It believed that Wake Forest kept its part of the contract but Gregg did not. It reasoned that he was not injured and could have met his obligation. Failing to do so was a violation of the agreement he signed.

For years the National Collegiate Athletic Association (herein referred to as NCAA) enforced a regulation known as the 1.6 Rule. The Rule, in part, states:

> A member institution shall not be eligible to enter a team or individual competitors in an NCAA sponsored meet, unless the institution in the conduct of all its intercollegiate athletic programs:
>
> > limits . . . eligibility for participation in athletics or in organized athletic

practice sessions during the first year in residence to student-athletes who have a predicted minimum grade point average of at least 1.6 (based on a maximum of 4,000) as determined by the Association's national prediction tables or Association-approved conference or institutional tables.[5]

In January of 1973 the NCAA, at its Annual Convention held in Chicago, amended the 1.6 Rule. The amendment will be effective in 1974-75 and will require a 2.0 grade average from a high school graduate. The 1.6 Rule was based on class rank and scores on the SAT or ACT test. Needless to say, the new rule will be much easier for high school graduates to attain than the 1.6 Rule.

In the present case eleven student-athletes failed to predict the 1.6 average required under NCAA regulations. These students qualified for admission to California State University at Sacramento (herein referred to as CSUS) under a "four percent rule." The "four percent rule" enabled the University to admit students without taking the SAT or ACT test. The students could be "admitted on the basis of such factors as economic need, motivation and maturity." CSUS officials felt that the eleven athletes met these standards and possessed the ability to successfully pass college work.

Schools that did not abide by the NCAA 1.6 Rule could not compete for national championships, appear on TV or in post season events. CSUS decided that it wanted to participate in all the events above and chose to adhere to the 1.6 Rule.

Due to several factors that appear to be inadvertent and not intentional, the University reported that all eleven athletes were eligible under the NCAA rules. In reality, however, none of the eleven were eligible. At the end of the freshman year all eleven had attained at least a 1.6 grade average and were making satisfactory academic progress at CSUS.

When CSUS realized that a violation had occurred, it reported the facts to the NCAA. The NCAA strongly recommended that CSUS declare the eleven athletes ineligible. The institution had two choices in the matter, (1) declare the athletes ineligible for one year, (2) face NCAA action. It therefore ruled that the eleven athletes were ineligible for athletic participation for one year. The NCAA followed by putting CSUS on probation for two years but permitted NCAA participation during this time.

The athletes instituted a suit requesting relief by arguing that the NCAA 1.6 Rule is:

> (1) unreasonably discriminatory and there-
>   fore in violation of the Fourteenth
>   Amendment to the United States
>   Constitution, and
> (2) denies plaintiffs their right to freedom
>   of association in violation of the First
>   Amendment to the United States
>   Constitution.

The United States District Court considered the

issue to be the question of whether the 1.6 Rule "results in an unreasonable classification, in violation of the Equal Protection Clause of the Fourteenth Amendment to the United States Constitution." The court then asked the question, is there "state action"? It concluded that there was by citing *Parish v. NCAA* [6] in which the court said,

> .... We must and do conclude that there definitely is state action here, in the constitutional sense, when NCAA regulates schools and universities at least half of which are public.

The court then tackled another fundamental question by asking if "the classification here complained of can measure up to equal protection standards."

The defendant NCAA explained the purpose of the 1.6 Rule which was intended:

(1) to reduce the possibility of exploitation of young athletes through the recruiting of athletes who would not be representative of the institution's student body and probably would be unable to meet the necessary academic requirements for a degree,

(2) to foster and preserve the concept of college athletics as sport engaged in by athletes who were first and primarily students, and

(3) to recognize the possibility that any student who could not meet the requirements of the 1.6 Rule should not engage in athletics during his

freshman year but should devote his
full time to study.

The California Court concerned itself with the
"interpretation which creates a classification which
does not conform to equal protection requirements."
It set up a new classification for students, such as
the eleven athletes at CSUS, who while not
predicting a 1.6 average, practiced and played during
their freshman year and were then denied a year's
participation for doing so. The court disputed the
logic of penalizing an athlete who achieves a 1.6
after a year because he failed to predict that average
previously. The key statement from the Court
appears to be the reasoning that:

> As each of the individual plaintiffs in this
> case had earned at least a 1.600 grade point
> average at the end of his freshman year at
> CSUS, the 1.600 rule of the NCAA as
> interpreted, is in violation of the Equal
> Protection Clause and is therefore
> unconstitutional insofar as it seeks to
> declare these student athletes ineligible for
> future intercollegiate participation based
> on the fact that they (1) failed to predict a
> 1.600 grade point average prior to entrance
> to CSUS and (2) practiced and/or competed
> in intercollegiate athletics during their first
> year in attendance at CSUS.

The Court then made an interesting observation
that is worth quoting regarding athletic
participation. It clearly conveyed its attitude by
remarking that:

> the opportunity to participate in
> intercollegiate athletics is a fleeting one. A

student can compete for a maximum of only four years and then his college career is over. During those four brief years, the athlete is afforded the opportunity to compete and work with others, to gain confidence in himself, and to mature emotionally and physically. Also, it cannot be overlooked that many college athletes lay the foundation for a rewarding professional athletic career during their four years of intercollegiate competition. In this day and age of professional sports, Olympic games, and the like, it cannot be denied that college athletics can be of the utmost importance to many student-athletes.

The Court concluded by ruling that two of the athletes were granted the injunction to participate while nine of the other athletes had already passed through the year of ineligibility and were now eligible to play.

United States Justice Thomas McBride wrote a letter to a fellow judge in Oklahoma. In the letter he briefly explained his reasoning behind the decision in this case. He ended his letter by writing that "I am not sure that I have answered all of my own questions, but at least I can sleep with my decision."

This decision represented a serious blow to the NCAA and its 1.600 Rule. The case was appealed to the United States Court of Appeals for the Ninth Circuit and in March, 1974 was reversed in favor of the NCAA.[6.1]

The higher court considered all the testimony and

findings summarized above and made its decision
for the following reasons:

1. The 1.600 Rule is not an unreasonable
   classification nor is it a violation of the
   Equal Protection Clause of the Constitution.
2. The NCAA adopted the rule in an
   attempt to reduce the exploitation of
   athletics who might be recruited just to
   participate in athletics without regard
   to their academic ability.
3. The 1.600 Rule is related to the purpose for which it was enacted in a reasonable manner.
4. The Rule would be destroyed if some
   penalty was not imposed. To meet the
   objective of the Rule, eligibility must be
   determined at the time of the student's
   application.

The Appellate Court, therefore, reversed the lower
court's order to grant the plaintiffs a preliminary
injunction.

In addition to cases against regulatory bodies, a
new era has developed in which state and federal
legislators are becoming involved in athletics. The
Amateur Athletic Act (Omnibus Bill) or (S. 2365),
the Devine or (H.R. 9171), the Teague or (H.R. 8989)
or Dellums Athletic Safety Act (H.R. 2575), will
certainly give athletics a new look if passed. The
Comparative Analysis of Senate, House Sports Bills
is reproduced here for the reader's convenience.

A sampling of three proposed bills will indicate

the intent of legislators regarding legislation and athletics.

Amateur Athletic Act of 1973

For years the NCAA and AAU have been feuding over the control of amateur athletics in the United States. Many charges and countercharges have been aimed at the various governing bodies throughout the years. The arguments have been made that insist that individual athletes have been punished by the "internecine warfare between competing sports governing bodies." [7]

A group of United States Senators led by John Tunney of California have proposed the Amateur Athletic Act of 1973 (also referred to as the Senate Omnibus). The Act would create a five-man board to supervise international athletic competition such as the Pan American Games and the Olympics. [8]

The Act has, oddly enough, caused the warring organizations to join forces to fight the inclusion of such an Act into federal law.

Philip Krumm, President of the United States Olympic Committee, denounced the Act as a threat to the rights of amateur athletes while David Rivens, the AAU president, predicted an end to the AAU and the thousands who volunteer their services to amateur athletics. He went on record as being "absolutely opposed to any control on the part of the federal government." [9]

The assistant to the Executive Director of the NCAA also opposed any federal intervention in amateur athletics and urged that any control be kept to a "minimum." [10]

Senator Tunney acknowledged the uproar and criticism by observing that he expected it because the Act puts the pressure on the governing bodies and threatens their authority. Tunney deplored the lack of representation on the various organizations and stated that one of the features of the new Act would be to give athletes, who are really at the center of things, the chance to be represented in decision-making. [11]

Athletes, in general, support the Act but fear that national administration of athletics may tend to promote even more nationalism, in games such as the Olympics, than ever before. [12]

Harold Connelly, former Olympic gold medal winner, praised the intent of the bill for its desire to include the athlete in policy making. He also felt

that the bill could provide much needed funds to promote athletic programs. Under the Act, the federal government would match funds raised by the foundation up to 50 million dollars.[13]

Specific goals mentioned in the Amateur Athletic Act of 1973 are:

   (1) fundamental reform of the United States Olympic Committee;
   (2) an end to disputes among organizations which govern amateur sports in this country, and
   (3) federal assistance for the development of amateur sports and physical fitness.[14]

The Act is intended to meet these goals by specifying that:

Title I of the Act would establish the United States Amateur Sports Board to insure that private organizations which control amateur sports and which purport to represent the citizens of the United States are responsive to the needs of amateur athletics and the public at large.

Title I would also authorize a study of the United States Olympic Committee, a private corporation, chartered by an Act of Congress to represent the United States in the Olympic Games.

Title II would create a National Sports Development Foundation to grant development funds to enhance a broad-based program of amateur sports and physical fitness.

The Athletic Safety Act (H.R. 2575).

The Occupational Safety and Health Act of 1970 (herein referred to as OSHA) was passed into law to help the states develop safeguards that would prevent serious injuries and loss of life to its workers.[15]

OSHA has provision to impose stiff penalties on all offenders with fines ranging from $1,000 to $10,000 for violation of OSHA standards. Employers who fail to remedy a cited violation can be assessed $1,000 per day until the situation is remedied.

OSHA standards are detailed and thorough regarding investigations, inspections, record keeping, penalties and judicial review.

Ronald V. Dellums, House of Representatives from California, has introduced H.R. 2575 for legislative approval. Dellums' bill is intended to amend OSHA as follows: [16]

    (1) by expanding OSHA coverage to every participant in an athletic contest between secondary schools or between institutions of higher education (as defined in section 801 of the Elementary and Secondary Education Act of 1965);

    (2) by regarding each such secondary school and institution of higher education as an "employer" of an individual representing that school or institution as a participant in an athletic contest;

    (3) by expanding the definition of national consensus standards to include for any

athletic contest the code of the NCAA
or the code of another recognized
national athletic organization for
institutions of higher education, any
recognized national athletic organization for secondary schools, or any recognized State Athletic organization
for such schools or institutions.
But if more than one code applies to
any such contest, the Secretary
shall designate as applicable to such
contest the code which assures the
greatest protection of the safety or
health of the affected participants.[17]

Participation is defined in the amendments to
OSHA as:

    (A) an athletic game, meet, bout, match
        or similar physical competitive meet-
        ing between teams or individuals rep-
        resenting at least two secondary
        schools or at least two institutions
        of higher education;
    (B) any practice or other preparation
        for such a meeting; or
    (C) any transportation to such a meet-
        ing or practice, or preparation
        provided for any participant of such
        contest by such school or institution
        which the participant represents.[18]

The Act then interprets its definition of a
participant as any individual:

    (A) who competes in any such meet-
        ing against such other institution or
        school;
    (B) who is a member of a team that so
        competes or a member of such team

> during any practice or preparation for
> any such meeting; or
> (C) who is a coach, trainer, manager,
>   or similar supporting individual of
>   such team or individual which com-
>   petes.[19]

The Athletic Care Act of 1973

Dellums intends also to introduce another bill
before Congress that will protect the health of a
participant in athletics. The Athletic Care Act of
1973, if implemented, will require a certified trainer,
within eight years after it is enacted into law, in
every school that participates in athletic
competition. Failure to provide such a trainer would
cause the Office of Education to stop the school from
such competition.[20]

Dr. L. W. Combs in 1971 stated that:

> of the approximately 25,000 high schools in
> the country, of which about 60% sponsor
> football programs, only about 100 schools
> employ the services of a full-time
> teacher-athletic trainer.[21]

The ramifications of the proposed legislation are
tremendous. Truly, if adopted by Congress, the new
laws will make athletics "a whole new ballgame."

Title IX of the Education Amendments of 1972

One of the most significant legislative acts in
recent years, with strong implications for women in
sports, was enacted in 1972. Title IX of the
Education Amendments states:

> No person in the United States shall, on the
> basis of sex, be excluded from participation
> in, be denied the benefits of, or be subjected

to discrimination under any education program receiving federal financial assistance.[22]

The act covers:

Preschools, elementary and secondary schools, institutions of vocational education, professional education, and undergraduate and graduate higher education.

Title IX includes any program that benefits from federal assistance. It does exempt, however, certain military institutions or church-affiliated colleges that limit or prohibit participation based on sex due to religious beliefs.[23]

Title IX has special implications for women in athletics. Some of the provisions of the Act that affect women include: [24]

Comparable facilities

A recipient shall provide comparable tiolet, locker room, and shower facilities for the different sexes, but may provide such facilities separately for members of each sex.

Access to education program or activity
Course offerings:

A recipient shall not provide any course or otherwise carry out any of its education program or activity separately on the basis of sex, or require or refuse participation therein by any of its students on such basis, including health, physical education, industrial, business, vocational, technical, and home economics courses.

Athletics

A. General:

Except as provided in this section, no person shall, on the basis of sex, be excluded from participation in, be denied the benefits of, be treated differently from another person, or otherwise be discriminated against in any athletic program or activity operated by a recipient, and no recipient shall provide any such program or activity separately on such basis. In complying with this paragraph, a recipient shall offer instruction and activities in sports in which members of both sexes have demonstrated a desire to participate.

B. Competitive Athletics defined:

1. For the purposes of this section, "competitive athletics" means all athletic teams operated by a recipient, selection for which is based upon competitive skill, including all training, coaching, and other activities related thereto.

2. For the purpose of this section:

   i. all competitive intramural or other athletics conducted during such competitive athletic season among teams operated by a single recipient, or by a single school operated by a recipient which is a local educational agency, will be considered a single competitive athletic program; and

   ii. all competitive athletics conducted during each competitive season between teams operated by a re-

cipient, or by a school operated
by a recipient which is a local
educational agency, and teams
operated by any other school,
college, university, or other entity
(whether or not a recipient) will
be considered a single competitive athletic program, regardless of whether such athletics
are conducted at the freshman,
junior varsity, club, or other level.

C. Competitive Athletics Generally
   A recipient which operates a competitive
athletic program:
1. shall do so without discrimination on the basis of sex, and shall
   provide students of each sex an
   equal opportunity to participate
   therein;
2. shall not discriminate therein on the
   basis of sex in the provision of equipment or supplies, scheduling of
   games and practice times, travel
   and per diem allowance, award of
   athletic scholarships, opportunity to
   receive coaching and instruction, provision of locker room and medical
   facilities and services, publicity or
   otherwise; and
3. shall, with regard to members of a
   sex, for which competitive athletic
   opportunities previously have been
   limited, make affirmative efforts to:
   i. determine in what sports members
      of each sex would desire to com-
      pete, and whether or not in
      teams conducted separately on
      the basis of sex;

ii. provide competitive athletic opportunities in which sports and through such teams; and

iii. inform members of such sex of the availability for them of competitive athletic opportunities equal to those available for members of the other sex.

D. Participation in Competitive Athletics

A competitive athletic program operated by a recipient, or by a school operated by a recipient which is a local educational agency, in which a higher proportion of all students of one sex than of all students of the other sex participate but which otherwise complies with this part, will be considered in compliance with this section if such recipient or school demonstrates to the satisfaction of the Director, upon his or her request that:

1. the higher proportionate participation by members of one sex reflects greater interest in competitive athletics on the part of all students of that sex as a group; and

2. the lower proportionate participation by members of the other sex does not reflect discrimination on the basis of sex in selection or recruitment for participation in competitive athletics, or in the selection of competitive sports.

E. Separate Competitive Teams

1. A recipient which operates compe-

titive athletics may, in any particular sport, operate separate teams for each sex, or a single team for which members of each sex are selected without discrimination on the basis of sex.

2. If such recipient operates such a single team, in a particular sport, and if substantially more members of one than the other sex are selected for such team, such recipient shall provide comparable opportunities to participate in the same sport or other sports, for members of such other sex, to the extent necessary to comply with paragraphs (c) and (d).

Charlotte Hallum predicts that schools at all levels will be forced by the provisions of Title IX to no longer require: [25]

all male or all female students to take specific classes, unless students of both sexes are required to take the classes. (For example, home economics may not be required for girls unless it is also required for boys.)

She also foresees budgets which will provide equal facilities for both sexes. Hallum believes female and male teams will continue to exist but some girls will undoubtedly compete on male teams while some males compete on female teams. The chief difference will be that schools will now make certain that both girls and boys have the opportunity for equal competition in athletics.[26]

IN MY OPINION

Let's look at athletic scholarships and the problems they present. Many years ago a major college football team had some outstanding young freshmen and sophomores that were inexperienced but destined for promising futures. Unfortunately the coach could not wait for the luxury of time. When a dozen or more former players returned from service, he decided to remedy his problem. At every position where former players were returning to give him the needed depth, he mailed a penny postcard to the young and sometimes not as talented football players, discontinuing their athletic scholarships. Not only did he cut their grant off, he did not take the time to call his men in and explain the reason for his action. No one sued, no one thought they could . . . such were the times in which we lived. In a climate such as this many things that violate decency and fair play were permitted.

Because of situations like this, the NCAA, while meaning well, and because it tried so hard to protect the student-athletes, set policies that at times were unrealistic.

I attended an NCAA meeting in Los Angeles and heard officials say that an athlete could be awarded a grant, decide after a few practices that football or other sports interfered with his studies and force the school to keep him on the grant for four years.

I remember turning to the Commissioner of a large conference and asking in total disbelief, "Can this actually happen"? "Not only can it happen," he said, "but it does."

I think this rule caused many student-athletes

to take advantage of athletic departments all over the United States. While the rule was to protect the athlete from an unscrupulous coach, it did little to protect the coach and school from an athlete who wanted to take the easy way out. In either case both situations were immoral!

Recently the NCAA and other such organizations realized the difficulty certain rules put on the institutions and made adjustments that are logical and sensible. Today an athletic grant can be awarded for one year at a time. The student-athlete can't lose his grant at the whim of a coach, however, since a loss of a grant must be taken before the faculty committee that administers all students grants.

At last we appear to be on a safe road with policy that is fair. Such a case was tested in 1967 and the court upheld the decision of the institution.

In like manner, the court considered a situation in which an institution erred and not the athletes and refused to uphold the penalty imposed by the school and its governing body. Truly, athletes are protected today as never before.

It is becoming apparent that advocates of athletics are divided on the effect that Title IX of the Education Amendments of 1972 will have on amateur sports.

One group favors the Act and feels that it is the salvation of women's athletics and the way to correct past injustices.

Another group led by Robert James, Commissioner of the Atlantic Coast Conference and Walter Byers, Executive Director of the powerful NCAA, agrees that such legislation will be detrimental to amateur athletics. Opponents of the Act believe that its guidelines will create chaos for all sports programs.

Certainly the 1970's will be crucial to all amateur sports programs and such legislation as Title IX will provide far-reaching and serious efforts upon both male and female athletic programs.

1. *The Review of the News,* August 22, 1973.
2. *Id.*
3. *Id.*
4. Taylor v. Wake Forest Univ., 191 S.E.2d 379 (N.C. 1972).
5. Associated Students, Inc., of California State Univ. v. NCAA, Civil Case No. S-2754 (Cal. 1973).
6. Parish v. NCAA, 361 F. Supp. 1220 (La. 1973).
6.1. Associated Students, Inc. of California State Univ. v. NCAA, No. 73-2278 (9th Cir. 1974).
7. *The Amateur Athletic Act of 1973.* Report of the Senate Committee on Commerce, [S. 2365] U.S. Government Printing Office, Washington, D.C., 1973.
8. Greensboro Daily News, July 16, 1973.
9. *Id.*
10. *Id.*
11. *Id.*
12. *Id.*
13. *Id.*
14. *The Amateur Athletic Act, supra* note 7.
15. *Public L. No. 91-596,* [S. 2193] (Dec. 29, 1970).
16. JOHN O'NEILL, COMING: TWO BILLS FOR SCHOOL SPORTS SAFETY, Kendall Sports Trail, May-June, 1973.
17. *Id.*
18. *Id.* at 7.

19. *Id.*
20. Kendall Sports Trail, *supra* note 16.
21. *Id.*
22. Charlotte Hallum, *Legal Tools to Fight Sex Discrimination, Phi Delta Kappan,* Vol. LV, No. 2, October, 1973.
23. *Id.* at 129.
24. Title IX of the Education Amendments of 1972. Department of Health, Education and Welfare, § 86.24, § 86.33, § 86.38.
25. Hallum, *supra* note 22 at 130.
26. *Id.*

8. Quick Kicks!

*Her bikini was a distracting
and disruptive influence.*[1]

There are various cases regarding athletics that do not fall into a fixed category. While these cases may not be many in number, they do represent cases that are interesting and informative. They may offer the possibility of new trends in athletic law that may become precedent setting, landmark cases.

New York Commissioner of Education Decides Two Issues

Can a junior high school physical education teacher be forced to teach swimming in a specified bathing suit? Can the same teacher, if she so chooses, wear a two-piece bathing suit that is commonly known as a "bikini" to class?

Much discussion and unhappiness occurred when Heather Martin was directed to stop teaching her physical education swimming class of junior high school boys in a bikini.[2] Ms. Martin was told by her superintendent and principal that her "bikini" revealed too much and was a "distractive influence" on her class that "interfered with the teaching and learning process" of her class.

Ms. Martin, a tenured teacher in New York, disputed the charges by protesting the directive as a violation of her personal rights and freedom. The respondents answered her by stating that they in no way were dictating dress standards but merely trying to operate the school as best they could. They insisted that their regulation was essential for "the smooth administration, operation and discipline of the school."

The athletic director testified that Ms. Martin was a good disciplinarian who had control at all times of her classes.

The Commissioner of Education supported the

practice of any employer setting a reasonable dress code for the employees. In this instance, however, he felt that the principal and superintendent were basing their argument on the belief that her "bikini" was "a distracting and disruptive influence."

He, therefore, ordered the administrators to set the regulation aside and permit the physical education teacher to wear her bikini if she so desired.

The New York Commissioner then decided another case that came to him. Many people become earnestly interested in high school athletics and try to influence public opinion at times of controversy. Many schools encourage touchdown clubs and booster clubs to raise necessary funds to promote athletics in the community. Most so-called booster clubs do tremendous good for the athletes, the coaches, and the school itself. Occasionally such organizations become involved with the hiring and firing of personnel and can and do become powerful pressure groups that can become disruptive to the total educational program of the school.

Two coaches were relieved of their responsibilities in football and the local touchdown club appealed the action to the Commissioner.[3] While no reasons were outlined in the Commissioner's decision, one point was made very clear.

The matter of appeal belongs to the person involved and not the parents or interested patrons of the school. The Commissioner referred to a previous case in *Matter of Phieffer* (Ed. Dept. Rep. 160, 1958), in which the parents of the school district attempted to appeal a school district decision regarding teaching personnel. The Commissioner answered the parents' appeal by ruling that:

> A member of the teaching staff of the district who feels that his legal rights have been contravened by action of the board would have a right of appeal from such action. However, it has been pointed out on many occasions in the past that other persons, such as voters or taxpayers of the district, are not aggrieved parties within the meaning of section 310 of the Education Law and hence have no standing to bring such appeals.

The Commissioner answered the appeal of the Sachem Touchdown Club by affirming his previous decision which he ruled similar and applicable to the present case. Certainly the coaches could appeal, but not the touchdown club, was the Commissioner's verdict.

An important case occurred in Sheboygan, Wisconsin, when William Richards, a high school basketball coach, was rehired as a teacher but not as a coach.[4] Richards had been a teacher of driver education and a cross-country coach and basketball coach since 1965. In 1970-71 he received $10,472 for teaching and a supplement of $980 for his duties as a basketball coach. His new contract stipulated a base salary of $11,475 for the 1971-72 year.

When Richards was told that he would not be rehired as the basketball coach he asked for a hearing so he could determine the reason for the nonrenewal of his basketball job. After numerous meetings and much discussion the plaintiff sought an injunction that would prohibit the defendants from hiring a new coach until his lawsuit was settled.

Richards argued that his coaching termination constituted a violation of due process according to the guaranteed rights of the Fourteenth Amendment. He also questioned the authority of the school board to dismiss him without a statement that would specify the reasons for failing to rehire him as the basketball coach.

The Supreme Court of Wisconsin referred to a Wisconsin case regarding a librarian in which it was pointed out that:

> in the absence of tenure rights the right to hire carries the concomitant of the right to fire. This power may be exercised by the board arbitrarily and without cause.[5]

The court in the Richards case considered important the fact that the school board and superintendent made no accusations or charges that would damage the plaintiff's reputation in the community or hamper him when he attempted to get a similar job in the future. It also reasoned that Richards was hired as a teacher and that his position as coach was one that did not require a certificate.

The Wisconsin Court then concluded that the defendants did not violate Richards' rights of due process since they renewed his teaching contract under similar terms of his past contract. It felt that his co-curricular duties did not come under the same conditions as his teaching assignment.

The decision of the lower court was affirmed and the temporary injunction previously given was vacated.

Student Fees Challenged

In recent years students on college campuses have begun to challenge the legality of certain fees that are required of them. Students who have little or no interest in athletics argue that only those who attend athletic contests should be required to pay an athletic fee. Still others claim that they do not read the school newspaper and should not be charged with a fee to support the paper. The argument goes on and on to varying degrees of intensity on most campuses.

The University of South Carolina wanted to expand and improve the football stadium and sought a method to do so. The General Assembly of South Carolina in 1970 passed an Act that gave the Board of Trustees of the University the authorization to issue "special obligation bonds" that would provide five million dollars for Carolina Stadium. The Trustees decided to add a specific fee of all regular, full-time, degree seeking students exclusive of summer school.

Richard Moye and his father sued the University's Board of Trustees and the Attorney General of South Carolina.[6] The Moyes claimed that enlarging a football stadium was certainly not an educational function. They also pointed out that the Act violated Act X, Sec. 1 of the South Carolina Constitution that required uniform and equal taxation. The plaintiffs then used the argument that is becoming familiar on campuses today, when they reasoned that they do not use the facility, or attend the games, so why pay fees? They also contended that Carolina Stadium was large enough for the entire student body, so why enlarge it?

The Supreme Court of South Carolina stated very forcefully that:

> A university, by its very nature, is a highly diversified institution whose aim is the highest development, mentally, morally and physically, of those who repair there to pursue excellence in their chosen fields. Indeed, one of the widely recognized criteria for judging the quality of a university is the breadth of activities, academic, social and athletic which it is able to offer both its students and the state of which it is an integral and vital part. The modern university is a monument to the ideas that the greatest benefit will be derived when men are free to choose among a variety of possible pursuits, to follow those which they find appealing, and to test themselves and their ideas in an atmosphere of tolerance and cooperation . . . .

The South Carolina Court then referred to a Texas case,[7] in which students objected, but were overruled, for challenging the payment of fees to the student union. The South Carolina Court then quoted an Iowa Court [8] that rejected a similar plea by students against fees. The Iowa Court made its position on student fees very clear when it asserted vigorously that:

> the fact that a student may not participate or take advantage of every facility available does not mean that he is or should be relieved from paying student fees allocated to various projects.

The South Carolina Supreme Court concluded its reasoning by deciding that the court could not substitute its judgment for that of the General Assembly or Board of Trustees. It left the decision up to those in authority. It found the charges of denial of equal protection and violation of the South Carolina Constitution to be out of order. Finally it answered the argument, set forth by the plaintiff, that the stadium was adequate for the student body by determining that:

> Students are not the only people to whom seating may properly be made available. Parents and family of students, their friends, alumni and their families and friends, faculty, staff, supporters, and opponents have an interest in attending games. And they too help finance the stadium out of their admission fee.

The Court supported the verdict of the lower court by reaffirming the authority of the legislature and Board of Trustees to improve and enlarge Carolina Stadium.

Kenneth Stringer sued Samuel Gould, the Chancellor of the State University of New York, because Stringer was required to pay a student activity fee to support extra-curricular activities.[9]

A resolution had been passed in 1968 by the Board of Trustees of the State of New York regarding student activity fees. The resolution enabled the various student bodies at the different state campuses to assess themselves with an annual fee that would support the various programs that its elected student government would approve.

All students were required to pay the fee and if any failed to pay the activities fees, the university officials were expected to withhold the student's grades and transcripts. Prior to the mandatory fee, students had paid a voluntary fee.

The various student governments requested that they administer the activity fee. The New York Court disagreed, however, and ruled that the trustees, not the student governments, should set the guidelines for the distribution of the funds. It ruled that the trustees had the responsibility to give guidance to the student groups as to how the funds were to be disbursed.

The court concluded that if the school could withhold grades and transcripts for failure to pay the fee which was set by the trustees, the trustees were in fact responsible for the distribution of the activity fees.

Lillian Bond and Daniel Fusfield sued the public schools of Ann Arbor, Michigan, in 1970 because the schools charged fees for books and supplies.[10] The pair wanted to force the Michigan schools to enroll all children without charging any fees at all. The plaintiffs freely admitted that they realized no one was denied admission to school because he or she could or did not pay fees. The fees, it was reported, were collected and put in a general fund for use just as tax revenues were used.

The plaintiffs insisted that the school district could not charge fees for courses such as "photography, art, home economics, and industrial arts, and the imposition of interscholastic athletic fees."

The Michigan Court concurred with the plaintiffs and ruled that the general fees were illegal and denied the Ann Arbor School District the right to collect fees in the future for books and supplies since they were obligated to furnish them for the operation of a free public school system.

It also ruled that the school district was in error when it charged fees for interscholastic athletics.

A final case regarding fees is one that has several interesting aspects in it.[11]

Dan and Kirk Paulson, through their father, sued the Minidoka County School District for its failure to forward a transcript of their grades to a college because they refused to pay a fee set by the School District's Board of Trustees. The required fee was $25.00 and covered various items, including an activity fee.

In 1968 the Board changed the schedule of fees as follows:

Textbook Fee.....................$12.50

School Activity Fee.............$12.50

The total of $25.00 remained the same. While the school would not take part payment of the $25.00 fee, it did not refuse a student who would not pay the fee the right to attend class. Nonpaying students were given textbooks without charge also.

Dan Paulson was given a cap and gown at graduation and received his diploma. The issue before the Idaho Court revolved around the fact that although Dan attended class, received books, diploma, cap and gown, etc., he was denied a copy of his academic transcript when he applied for admission to Idaho State University. The University of Idaho accepted him provisionally and he sued the school to secure his transcript.

The trial court decided that such a fee is unconstitutional and ordered the high school to supply Idaho State with a copy of Dan Paulson's transcript. The court based its ruling on previous decisions that ruled that Idaho schools were "free." In almost every case briefed with the exception of Utah, Washington, and South Dakota, the courts agreed with the "free" concept.

The question then arose as to the status of the activity fee which was used to pay for extracurricular activities. Since students are required to pay an activity fee whether they participate or not, the fee negates the "free" aspect

of the school. The court ruled that participation in
extracurricular activities is not essential for a high
school education. Therefore, the students who want
to engage in such activities can pay the fees. The
school could require payment of the activity fee
from anyone who participated in such activities.

Finally the court decreed that:

> the legal duty to make available a
> transcript arises from the practicality that,
> in our society, the ability to obtain a
> transcript without cost is a necessary
> incident of a high school education. A
> reasonable fee after the first free
> transcript, representing actual costs, would
> be proper and may be charged for the
> duplication and issuance of subsequent
> transcripts.

Defamation of Character

A. J. Foyt, the well-known race car driver,
recently sued *Sports Illustrated* for libel. Foyt,
according to the magazine, labeled fellow racers as
"hillbillies and fags." [12] The court upheld his claim of
innocence of the statement and awarded him $75,000
in damages.

Defamation of character cases are increasing
among coaches and athletes. While cases increase,
many people are still not certain of the meaning of
libel and slander and the basis of a lawsuit.

In *Public School Law*, Alexander, Corns, and
McCann treat the topic in depth. The authors
describe defamation by asserting that:

> the twin torts of libel and slander are based
> on defamation. Slander and libel consist of

false and intentionally published or communicated statements by one person which hold another person up to hatred, disgrace, ridicule, or contempt. If the statement is communicated by word of mouth or gestures, it is known as slander, if it is communicated in writing, printing, or pictures, it is libel. Simply stated, libel is written defamation and slander is oral defamation.[13]

The authors then clarified the court's attitude toward defamation by defining the feeling of the court:

Communication or publication means that the defamatory statements must have been made to one other than the defamed party. If you accuse a person to his face or write him a personal letter, these acts do not constitute a communication or publication unless a third party hears the remarks or reads the letter. A person who repeats or republishes the defamatory statements is liable even though he discloses the sources of his statements.

Finally, the writers added one more aspect of defamation by stating that:

in order to constitute the tort of libel or slander the following elements must be shown:
(1) a false statement concerning another was published or communicated;
(2) the statement brought hatred, disgrace, ridicule or contempt on another person;
(3) damages resulted from the statement.

However, damages need not be shown where the statement charges that a person committed a crime, that he has a loathsome disease, or that the person, if a woman, is unchaste. Also, it is unnecessary to prove actual damages if the false statement is so derogatory as to injure the person in his trade or business.

It is interesting to look at a case in Oklahoma with the above as a background.

The Pill That Can Kill Sports

Demmit Morris was a fullback on the great Oklahoma football teams of the 1950's.[14] He played on the Bud Wilkinson coached 1956 team that won all ten of its regular season games and climaxed the year with a victory in the Orange Bowl in Miami. Morris also played on the 1957 and 1958 Oklahoma teams.

Fawcett Publications, Inc., were the publishers of a magazine called "True" and Morris instituted a lawsuit against the publisher because of libelous statements that appeared in a 1958 edition of the magazine. The article was entitled "The Pill that Can Kill Sports" and charged the Oklahoma football team with the use of amphetamines and like drugs. In the article the writer said:

> You can go to jail for selling amphetamine to a truck driver or injecting it into a racehorse, yet this same drug is being

handed out to high school and college athletes all over the country.

The article also had pictures of a truck in which two persons were labeled "Avarice and Ignorance shoveling out dope to athletes, including football players, who are running behind the truck and catching pills."

The truck has a sign on it that says "Dope" and on the truck are the words, "Victory at any cost."

The author then made a statement that was later challenged by Morris in court, when he said:

> Speaking of football teams, during the 1956 season, while Oklahoma was increasing its sensational victory streak, several physicians observed Oklahoma players being sprayed in the nostrils with an atomizer. And during a televised game, a close-up showed Oklahoma spray jobs to the nation.

The article then continued to criticize what had been observed on television by commenting that:

> Ten years ago, when that was done to a horse, the case went to court. Medically, there is no reason for such treatment. If players need therapy, they shouldn't be on the field.

The magazine then continued to expound on the practice of users and characterized them in the following manner:

> the "lifter" can and does become heroic, boisterous, pugnacious, or vicious.

It then discussed some "brutal crimes" that had taken place throughout the United States by people who used the pills. It bitterly commented that:

> these results are what make amphetamines useful in the field of athletics. They promote aggressions, increase the competitive spirit, and work the same as epinephrine (adrenalin) produced in your body. The adrenalin cortex, however, is wiser than victory-hungry coaches and athletes.

The plaintiff considered the statements in the nationally published magazine to be damaging to all the members of the Oklahoma team and took exception to them. He produced evidence that substantiated the fact that the team used "spirits of peppermint" to relieve a common condition that existed among football players in hot weather, known as "dry mouth" or "cotton mouth." The spray was simply a means of helping this condition and no proof was supplied at the trial that proved that any Oklahoma football player was using pills or drugs of any type.

The defendant, Fawcett Publications, tried to defend the article by contending that:

(1) The article is not libelous per se:
   A. The plaintiff was not named or referred to in the article.
   B. No person understood or believed the article referred to the plaintiff.

    C. The article does not allege the
       plaintiff engaged in criminal activity
       and is not libel per se.
    D. Plaintiff is a member of a large
       and changing group class and
       therefore the article is not libel
       per se.

The court looked at the evidence that was brought forth during the trial and decided that it was defamatory in nature against the Oklahoma University football team. It felt that it certainly was conducive to ill feelings on the part of the readers toward the team members and destroyed public confidence in the team. The court then considered arguments as to what constituted libelous action brought by the defendant. It referred to many previous cases in which "class libel" and "group libel" were defined. In one case, the court held that one "member" of the Jewish race in Quebec, consisting of 75 families out of a total city population of 80,000 people, could maintain an action of defamation of the entire group even though he was not assailed individually, but only as a member of the group.[15]

On the other hand, other cases stated that when a group was mentioned the person suing must prove that the charge applied to him if action were to be maintained.[16]

The court, while not unanimous in its decision, did rule that Fawcett Publications, Inc., was guilty of libelous action and awarded Demmit Morris $75,000 in damages. It affirmed the decision of the lower court in favor of the plaintiff.

Peter Kondos was hired for one year as assistant football coach at Marshall University.[17] The coach claimed that President Roland Nelson "did libel and slander the plaintiff." Kondos claimed that Nelson knew that his statements were untrue and that he (Kondos) lost his reputation and good name in the coaching field because of the slanderous remarks.

The West Virginia court, however, ruled that Nelson was an agent of the Board of Regents and that Marshall University by being a state school enjoyed the protection of the governmental immunity doctrine. It ruled that Nelson was protected just as the Board of Regents when he terminated the contract of Coach Kondos.

Many people have raised the question regarding the use of public, municipal facilities by private schools that are racially segregated. A 1973 case in Alabama may serve as a guide for future cases.

Four private schools with all-white enrollments used the municipal stadium in Montgomery, Alabama, in 1971.[18] During the fall of 1971 approximately 14 games were played between all-white private schools while 16 games were played between public schools and one football game was conducted involving a Roman Catholic school which was racially desegregated.

A district court ruled in 1965 that the schools in Montgomery were violating the Fourteenth

Amendment by operating racially desegregated schools. It ordered immediate integration in the four grades for the fall term.

In 1969 the Department of Health, Education and Welfare was directed by the district court to devise a plan that would insure the elimination of a dual system of education.

The district court reasoned that the use of the public stadium aided the private schools in the following manner:

(1) the opportunity to play athletic contests in public facilities contributes considerably to the attractiveness of the all-white private schools and draws white students from public schools, thus increasing the difficulty of desegregating public education,

(2) The use of public facilities saves the capital outlay required to build similar facilities, and

(3) The City's action in granting the schools exclusive possession of city property for the duration of the contest provides a means by which the school can raise extra revenue through the sale of tickets and refreshments.

The district court decided that the use of the football stadium and other recreational facilities such as "baseball diamonds, basketball courts and tennis courts for official athletic contests and similar functions sponsored by racially segregated private schools" aided these schools and impaired the cause of the public school.

The U. S. Court of Appeals, Fifth Circuit, supported the attitude of the district court by ruling that it was within its jurisdiction to enjoin the officials of the City of Montgomery from providing the facilities of the City for usage by the private schools.

The Court of Appeals made a distinction, however, between the use of the stadium for a football game and the use of the public facilities for individuals or groups of children who happened to be enrolled in private schools. It emphatically stated that "the children enrolled in private schools have an unquestioned right as citizens to make use of municipal recreational facilities." The Court of Appeals then made an interesting observation when it commented that:

> permitting private school groups to enjoy such recreational facilities as zoos, museums, and parks or to attend, along with other citizens, civic and cultural events conducted in city recreational facilities does not involve the same degree of affirmative state action as granting exclusive control of public facilities for private school functions.

It distinguished between the various usage of public facilities by adding that:

> nonexclusive use of governmental facilities and services does not provide a means by which schools may raise revenue. No schools, public or private, were shown to have constructed or maintained facilities such as zoos, parks, and the like.

It concluded therefore that the use of the facilities by private school children did not pose a threat to the desegregation of public education.

The Court of Appeals then relied on a recent case that attracted much attention by its nature and significance.

In *Irvis* the United States Supreme Court in 1972 reversed a previous decision that prohibited the Moose Lodge from obtaining a license to sell liquor until it eliminated its alleged racial policy of discrimination.[19] The Supreme Court felt that the:

> State licensing of the Harrisburg Moose Lodge did not significantly affect the right of minority groups to purchase liquor or to obtain club licenses for themselves.

The Court of Appeals viewed the *Irvis* case as one in which a private club in a private building sought a license while in the present case the issue was the use of public supported and owned facilities for use by a private group.

It concluded that while the district court could enjoin the City of Montgomery from letting private all-white schools use its public facilities it should make a distinction in not denying the same conveniences to private school children or groups for nonexclusive use of its recreational facilities.

IN MY OPINION

It is interesting to note the variety of cases involving athletics and physical education that are reaching today's courts.

The New York Commissioner of Education along with his counterpart in New Jersey has decided many cases that relate to both athletics and physical education.

While New York and New Jersey seem to take a liberal attitude toward students' dress and appearance, they likewise observe personal freedom in both areas for their teachers. In some states a teacher's suspension because she wore a bikini bathing suit to a boys' swimming class would be upheld . . . but not in New York.

New York, however, took a different view when a booster club wanted to question the removal of two coaches from their coaching duties. While the Commissioner ruled that either or both coaches could appeal themselves, he objected to a group of parents or interested townspeople interfering, no matter how good the intentions might be, with school policy.

I remember as a young coach a particular interview in which I did not talk with the school principal. Instead he quickly shuttled me to a downtown store where the chairman of the board talked to me in glowing terms about the advantages of the job. He listed the many pluses that existed such as a talented and large number of athletes ready to play, eager for a championship under the proper coach. He mentioned town support, beautiful facilities, outstanding band, any type of equipment I needed. Then he talked salary and not only did he offer a substantial pay raise from my present job but such bonuses as a free home with any utilities I needed furnished and the opportunity to buy all my necessities such as a stove, refrigerator, etc., at a *very special low cost*. The man never asked my teaching qualifications but spent all his time emphasizing the benefits that I would receive if I could just WIN, WIN, WIN!

Needless to say, I turned it down and took a position at a school that offered only the legitimate salary and the best possible offer from the principal his support and that of the school board if I would work hard, teach well, coach effectively and abide by the rules. He did everything he said and a year later at the previous school I visited, one of the state's outstanding coaches was fired. I still wonder if the man at the corner store did the firing or if the unseen principal was given the honor of handling such an unpleasant chore.

Booster Clubs, Touchdown Clubs and similar organizations do a great job in most communities but when they are allowed to dictate the *hiring and firing* policy they become albatrosses around the neck of educators. The victims become losing coaches!

Certainly more policies and decisions such as the one by the Commissioner of Education in New York regarding outside interference should be followed.

The question of fees paid by students is a timely one that is beginning to receive judicial attention. For years, schools have claimed the name of the "free public school" and then charged fees for almost anything. It always bothered me that many economically deprived students were required to pay a typing fee, but there was not a special fee for Greek, Latin, Geometry for the college-bound student.

The court has said that no fee could be required if the school is a free public school and it prohibited a school from denying a student, who refused to pay a fee, a copy of his transcript for college admission.

Two coaches from different colleges boasted that any student on an athletic scholarship who transferred to another school would be forced to pay back the amount awarded him or be denied his transcript. The athlete was helpless and usually stayed on — today this could not stand up if challenged in court.

Two prominent and outstanding football coaches were put through a trying ordeal several years ago when a man's telephone call was inadvertently put into the same line as the coaches and he heard the discussion between the two. He interpreted the conversation as one in which the coaches were "fixing" the game and reported the incident to a national magazine. The magazine lost the case as did the one in the preceding chapter in which a team was accused of using drugs.

The court has made it quite clear that libel and slander will not be tolerated when the remarks, if not proven true, hurt the reputation of the person by holding him up to "ridicule, hatred, disgrace, or contempt."

It did, however, continue to protect agents of the state, such as board members and presidents of institutions, from such lawsuits by covering them with the umbrella of governmental immunity.

One thing is certain, the athlete and his role are public news and open to public scrutiny. Many of the injustices and ills will be corrected because people are now aware of what is happening.

1. In the Matter of the Appeal of Heather Martin (Decision No. 8156 of N.Y. Commissioner of Education, 1970).
2. *Id.*
3. In the Matter of the Appeal of Miguel Orrach (Decision No. 8338 of N.Y. Commissioner of Education, 1971).
4. Richards v. Board of Educ. Joint School Dist. No. 1, City of Sheboygan, 206 N.W.2d 597 (Wis. 1973).
5. Adamczyk v. Caledonia, 190 N.W.2d 137 (Wis. 1971).
6. Moye v. Board of Trustees of Univ. of South Carolina, 177 S.E.2d 137 (S.C. 1970).
7. Rainey v. Malone, 141 S.W.2d 713 (Tex. 1940).
8. Iowa Hotel Ass'n v. State Bd. of Regents, 114 N.W.2d 539 (Iowa 1962).
9. Stringer v. Gould, 314 N.Y.S.2d 309 (1970).
10. Bond v. Public Schools of Ann Arbor School Dist., 178 N.W.2d 484 (Mich. 1970).
11. Paulson v. Minidoka County School Dist. No. 331, 463 P.2d 935 (Idaho 1970).
12. *The Review of the News*, Sportsman, July 4, 1973, at 24.
13. K. ALEXANDER, R. CORNS, W. McCANN, PUBLIC SCHOOL LAW, West Publishing Co., St. Paul, Minn., 1969 at pp. 324-325.
14. Fawcett Publications v. Morris, 377 P.2d 42 (Okla. 1962).
15. Ortenberg v. Planamdon, Que. Ct. App., 35 Can. Law Times 262, American Ann. Cas. 1915 C. at. 347.
16. 23 L.R.A. n.s. 726.

17. Kondos v. West Va. Bd. of Regents, 318 F. Supp. 394 (S.D. W. Va. 1970).
18. Gilmore v. City of Montgomery, 473 F.2d 832 (5th Cir. 1973).
19. Moose Lodge No. 107 v. Irvis, 407 U.S. 163, 176, 92 S. Ct. 1965, 1973 (1972).

9. Injuries Aren't in the Budget

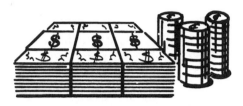

In spite of all the injuries on the gridiron, there seems to be no move to recall the human race because of the defective design of the kneebone.

Anonymous

Most coaches spend their time trying to devise ways to win ballgames. They spend hours talking about zones, attacking certain defenses, innovative ideas of offensive play and other aspects of the game.

Coaches spend little time thinking about lawsuits, costly trials, expensive damage awards, and the loss of professional status because of injuries.

Administrators do most of the worrying over the details that result in a lawsuit and countless days in court. The spiraling cost of litigation and the increasing number of suits involving coaches and physical education teachers cause real concern and an accompanying interest in preventing injuries.

The most frequent cause of litigation among teachers and coaches seems to evolve from alleged lack of supervision. A few cases can present the problem that confronts the average schoolman.

Supervision

It is generally agreed by educators that most school-related accidents could have been prevented with proper supervision. No one really expects teachers and coaches to provide instant and constant supervision to every student and athlete, but in many instances, more can be done to improve the situations that too often exist in our schools.

In California a group of students were walking toward the gymnasium during the lunch hour.[1] Several of the boys started to "slap box" and although no hard blows were exchanged, the plaintiff fell and fractured his skull. He died the following day.

The boy's parents sued the school because it failed to supervise the playground, contrary to California law which requires constant supervision. During the trial witnesses testified that the head of the physical education department had not assigned his staff members for supervisory duty.

Although the "slap-boxing" attracted over 30 spectators, the defendant teachers who were "talking on the telephone," working on lesson plans and eating lunch at the time failed to hear the noise.

The appellate court reversed the judgment of the lower court and favored the boy's parents. The court ruled that the school was guilty of negligence because it did not furnish supervision. It reasoned that the boy would not have been allowed to "slap box" if teachers had been present and would not have died as a result of his injuries.

Rita Segerman was a fourth grade teacher in the Rollingwood Elementary School in Maryland.[2] She left her class doing exercises while she went to the principal's office to look at a student's record. Mary Jones was doing exercises when a boy hit her with his foot causing her to lose two of her front teeth. Mary Jones and her father sued the teacher and the court granted her $5,000 and her father $1,130 for damages. As a result of the court's decision Segerman appealed the case to a higher court.

Segerman testified that the students were working on push-ups, sitdowns, and jumping jacks which were familiar to them. The boy who inadvertently kicked the plaintiff had left his assigned place against the instructions of his teacher.

The court relied on a statement from a book, *Tort Liability of Teachers*, as relative to this case. Paul Proehl, the author said:

> Broadly speaking, what is reasonable and what is foreseeable are the criteria in supervising classes. The standard is again one of "ordinary prudence." The impossible will not be required, although teachers know, it is often asked. Where supervision could not have prevented the injury, its lack will, of course, not be held to be the cause of the injury.[3]

The court then considered the following evidence:

(1) The class had previously done the exercises for at least a year in the physical education class.

   (2) The teacher played the record while the children were in their seats and then spaced them for their exercises.
   (3) She had no reason to believe that anyone would leave his assigned place on the floor.
   (4) The boy's action was not foreseeable by the teacher.

The court then pointed out that if a rule could be formulated regarding the liability of teachers, it would be:

> A teacher's absence from the classroom or failure to supervise students' activities is not likely to give rise to a cause of action for injury to a student, unless under all the circumstances the possibility of injury is reasonably foreseeable.[4]

The court, therefore, considered the controlling factor in the case to be the fact that the teacher could not foresee the action of the boy who kicked the plaintiff. For this reason, the court ruled that the defendant Rita Segerman was not negligent.

Terry Lueck was attempting a forward roll in the gymnasium when he fell after slipping on "a set of still rings."[5] Although Lueck had taken gymnastics in the physical education course for three years, he was still classified as an unskilled gymnast during his senior year.

The plaintiff and his physical education teacher agreed that he performed the exercise well on the still rings and that the forward roll was an elementary stunt that did not pose him any particular problems.

The court considered the facts regarding the supervision of the class and learned that the teacher conducted a two week orientation period, demonstrated the use of the apparatus, advised the class regarding rules of safety, and provided spotters for students attempting stunts.

An expert in the field of physical education testified that the supervision furnished by the teacher was adequate but that it "could have been more wisely handled with beginners."

The court surmised that the teacher provided adequate supervision and concluded that:

> The standard is what determines one's negligence and not what others might have personally done. A teacher should only be subjected to liability by the standards of care imposed and nothing more.

The teacher's conduct in the gymnastic class was upheld as not being negligent by the court.

A different decision was made by a New York Court that seems to oppose the Segerman and Lueck rulings. An eleven-year-old girl, Kathy Armlin, was injured during a physical education class in gymnastics.[6] Both parties disagreed as to the facts of the case but after an investigation the court ruled on the following information:

(1) Kathy stood up in the swings and fell on her back when she jumped out.
(2) She had seen other students dis-

mount in the same manner without the disapproval of her teacher.

(3) Her teacher told the class they could do anything they wanted to on the rings except swing and that they could get out of the rings by "going backwards so they could come down on their feet."

(4) The class had 35 girls in it and there were six different pieces of apparatus.

(5) Two students were assigned to spot for Kathy when she worked on the rings.

(6) The teacher never trained the spotters on how they were to perform and she never demonstrated the use of the proper exercises on the apparatus for the class.

At the time Kathy was injured, the teacher was at the trampoline and did not see the accident. The plaintiff referred to the State Physical Education Syllabus that specified that in a gymnastics class each piece of equipment needed to be placed so the teacher could view it all.

The trial court ruled that the teacher was negligent in her role as supervisor and the higher court affirmed the decision.

Unsupervised Gymnasiums

Morris Albers persuaded the school janitor to let a group of five boys in the gymnasium so they could play an informal basketball game during the Christmas holidays.[7] Morris and another boy played on the high school basketball team and were familiar with the gymnasium.

While the boys changed clothes Morris swept the gymnasium floor.

A loose ball was going out of bounds and Morris and another boy ran for it. Morris collided with the boy and hit his head on the other boy's hip and fell to the floor in a semi-conscious state. He spent considerable time in the hospital for a spinal fracture.

Morris claimed that the school district was at fault because it failed to provide supervision for the pick-up game. He also charged that the floor was dirty and they used a worn-out ball that they found near the equipment room.

The defendant school district answered the contention by arguing that it had no obligation to supervise an informal game during the holiday period. During the trial several witnesses testified that the school owed a duty to people who used the gymnasium at any time and had a responsibility to keep the facility in a safe condition.

The Idaho Court did not feel that the school district was negligent. It did not believe that a coach could have prevented the injury if he had been present. It observed that certain games offer normal contact, peculiar to the sport, and in this case, such contact was normal. It discounted the argument that the dirty floor contributed to the accident since Morris testified that he swept it before the group played.

It, therefore, supported the verdict of the trial court in favor of the school district.

One can visualize the attitude of the court if the floor had been defective or if a school official had granted the group permission to use the gymnasium if the games were known to be rough in nature. Although the court supported the school, care should be exercised in similar situations. A janitor or other member of the school staff should be instructed not to open the gymnasium unless directed to by the proper authorities.

Alan Kaufman, a nineteen-year-old student at Brooklyn College, was playing three-man basketball in the college gymnasium.[8] One of his opponents jumped for a ball at the same time Alan did, and a collision followed. Alan became unconscious and died soon after. The father of the deceased claimed that his son's death was a result of the unsafe condition of the gymnasium and a lack of supervision.

The testimony regarding the presence of instructors was in conflict at the trial but the court did not consider the absence or presence of supervisors important in this case. The New York Court concluded that such an accident could have happened no matter how many instructors were present. It felt that the accident was one that could occur just as well in the presence of the teacher as during his absence.

It reasoned that a lack of supervision was not the proximate cause of the accident. The court then referred to *Frazier v. YMCA* [9] in which a young boy of eight jumped up for a loose ball and hit the knee of an opponent during a basketball game. The court in the *Frazier* case said:

> In any event, there is no causal relation between the absence of a supervisor and the accident. Bodily contact is inherent in the game. There is no evidence which indicates that the "dribbling" and the "guarding" were done in any but the usual manner of the sport. The boy whose knee hit the plaintiff testified he did not mean to strike him. It does not appear how the presence of a supervisor during the play would have prevented the accident. It happened without warning and in the course of the play. The hazard of an accident resulting in injury is inherent in a game of basketball.

The court reasoned that if there was no liability in the above case, involving immature boys, it could find no negligence with mature, college age men. The case was dismissed in favor of the defendants.

Supervision for Extra-Curricular Activities

Many physical educators ask what the status is of intramural games and other extracurricular activities and supervision. While there aren't enough cases on record to provide a trend, one case gives some guidance on the subject.

Ira Rubtchinsky was told of a contest between the freshmen and sophomores called "Rivalry." [10] The game was endorsed by the officials of the State

University at Albany as a means of developing spirit among the classes. The members of the two classes had a choice between pushball or a banner hunt. Rubtchinsky decided to choose "pushball" after watching the way it was played. He was given the basic instruction in the techniques and fundamentals of the game.

During the game Rubtchinsky was hit from behind, such as clipping in football, and he sustained a painful and serious injury.

The University officials denied any responsibility for supervising the game but placed it on the Student Government who sponsored the extra-curricular activity. The plaintiff attempted to place the duty of supervision on the University since it still held the power of authority over the student organization.

The court considered the facts and then made several observations. First, it felt that the plaintiff was six feet tall and weighed 200 pounds and knew the rough nature of the game. It also believed that he was not compelled to participate, and when he did, he willingly assumed the inherent risks of the game.

The court then favored the University because it did not believe the school has the responsibility or duty for providing supervision to extra-curricular programs.

Lack of Competent Supervision

One of the most frequent charges in liability cases

is that of incompetent supervision. It is often difficult to determine competency in such cases and considerable testimony is required from so-called experts. The following case illustrates the contention of incompetence by litigants.

Eva Russell sued the officials of Morehouse College for the death of her son Arlee who drowned during a swimming class.[11]

Arlee enrolled in a swimming class which was required of all non-swimmers. The instructor of the class was responsible for teaching the course and supervising the group. He assigned several members of his swimming team to assist in the teaching of the class. Although they were good swimmers, none of them had passed the Red Cross Water Safety Instructors Course.

On the day of the fatal drowning, the instructor informed the class that two student assistants would handle the class. He then divided the class into two groups by ability.

The swimmers lined up at the deep end of the pool and were instructed to swim to the shallow end. Arlee was described as one who "struggled to keep afloat." He nevertheless lined up at the deep end and jumped into it with the other men who were capable swimmers.

He sank to the bottom of the pool and drowned.

It was three to five minutes before a swimmer spotted the body at the bottom of the pool. His body was retrieved by one of the student assistants who immediately administered artificial respiration.

The mother of the deceased made several charges against the physical education instructor and the college. She insisted that they were guilty of the following acts that resulted in negligent conduct:

(1) No such safe method of conduct for such instruction was prescribed, outlined, and specified by said defendant.

(2) Not knowing their ability to swim, they should have, in the exercise of ordinary care provided at least two trained and experienced instructors to watch and guard the members of said group while swimming.

The plaintiff also contended that the defendants:

(1) Failed to provide a swimming pool with adequate safeguards, adequate personnel and adequate rules for instructing the said class safely to prevent the drowning of any member thereof.

(2) Failed to place themselves in said swimming pool room where either could observe each member of said group while member was swimming from deep end to the shallow end.

The defendants charged Arlee with assuming the risk by attempting to swim in the deep end of the pool. Thus, they pointed out, he was guilty of contributory negligence.

The Georgia Court of Appeals disagreed that the plaintiff was guilty of either charge and actually felt that the defendants might have had a greater responsibility to him in a required class of physical education than it would to "a mere volunteer or trespasser."

The court answered a charge that the student assistant failed to revive the deceased by artificial respiration. It agreed that the student assistants were obligated to try to restore life in the stricken swimmer but insisted that:

> there was no duty upon them to be successful in such attempt.

The court ruled that the mother of the deceased child could sue the college for the death of her son. The college had claimed charitable immunity even though it owned an insurance policy for such liability.

Denise Driscol was in a girls physical education class that shared the gymnasium floor with a boys class.[12] Each class had a separate teacher. Denise's teacher usually dismissed the class from three to five minutes before the next period began. Denise had been in her class for three years and knew the procedure used. The girls class always waited for the boys class to leave before they would go to the shower room.

Denise ran toward the girls dressing room and tripped over the feet of another girl. As she fell, several other girls piled up on her causing her to crack her elbow and break her arm.

During the trial it was revealed that the school penalized those who were tardy by taking points from their academic grade. However, Denise had a lunch period following her physical education class and had no reason to run.

Denise listed several charges against the school and her teacher, Joyce Ghere.

She blamed them both for permitting 45 girls to attend class with only six shower stalls for such a large class. She accused the teacher of causing the accident by failing to give the class sufficient time to shower and get to the next class.

The Indiana Court did not uphold Denise's contention against her teacher since it remarked that the teacher had nothing to do with determining class size. It also stated that the teacher did not have a time minimum for the class set by the local or state authorities.

It also observed that the class was not subjected to unreasonable risk of injury because they ran to take showers. It emphasized this point by concluding:

> We therefore doubt that there is any unreasonable risk of injury involved in requiring high school students to run to their dressing room, whatever may be the requirement, so long as there are no unusual conditions (such as grease or water on the floor) present.

After considering all the testimony and facts before it, the Indiana Court favored the physical education teacher and the school.

Another Indiana case illustrates the thinking of the court regarding supervision after school.

Raymond Murray borrowed a bamboo pole from

his physical education teacher so he could practice high jumping on the weekend when school was not in session.[13]

Anita Bush and Raymond's sister returned to the school playground to ride bicycles. Anita watched Raymond jump and when his sister laughed when he missed a jump he became very angry. He threw the bamboo pole at his sister but hit Anita instead.

The injured girl sued the physical education teacher because he failed to supervise the area after school when a dangerous piece of equipment was used.

The court could not rule that the bamboo pole was dangerous at all. It reasoned that if the pole was dangerous, so was a "book, a board, or a bamboo fishing pole." If her argument was valid, each piece of such equipment would need constant supervision.

It dismissed the case against the physical education teacher.

Arthur Darrow sued the West Genesee Central School District for injuries he sustained during a physical education class.[14] The plaintiff was playing a game of line soccer in the gymnasium when he ran into a player on the opposing team. The teacher divided the class into two teams and gave each player a number that corresponded to one on the other team. The teacher would then call a number and the members of the team with such a number would run toward the ball and try to kick it through the opposing team.

The plaintiff claimed that the teacher did not give

the class adequate instructions or demonstrations and that this lack of proper instruction led to his injury. He furnished an expert who testified that a game of this type required reasonable care and instruction on the part of the teacher. He stated that the teacher should emphasize that in this game the boys:

> must play the ball as much as possible with their feet, without any bodily contact, that they should not charge the ball to the point of bringing about bodily contact and that there should be no pushing, shoving or rushing into each other.

The Supreme Court of New York considered the admission of the teacher that he did not instruct the boys as to what they should do when players arrived at the ball at the same time. For this reason it reversed the decision of the lower court in dismissing the complaint and ordered a new trial.

Sonny David Stanley was hit with a bat on the school playground during the summer recreation program. The trial court awarded him $40,000 in damages and the defendant appealed.[15]

The plaintiff charged the defendant with negligence for issuing a defective bat, "failing to warn the plaintiff and failure to supervise" the activity. The boy was hit by a bat that slipped out of a player's hand and struck him on the head. The summer recreation program was supervised by a qualified physical education teacher who was assisted by junior leaders. At the time of the accident, a seventeen-year-old assistant was supervising the playground. His responsibility was to make sure the younger children were not too near the older boys.

During the trial, testimony revealed that several games of fast pitch were in progress near the place where the plaintiff was playing. One of the fast pitch players got a bat from the school storeroom which had little or no tape on the handle. The plaintiff claimed that the distance between the area he occupied and the fast pitch games was dangerously close and that he should have been warned of the inherent danger that existed.

An expert witness testified that the plaintiff was too close to the fast pitch game for safety and was vulnerable to the flying bat that hit the boy. The defendants objected to the use of an expert witness in the case, but the court felt his testimony was in order. The higher court upheld the decision of the circuit court and favored the plaintiff.

Facilities and Equipment

James Scott was an outfielder on the baseball team at New York State Teachers College.[16] During an intercollegiate contest, he ran into a metal flag pole while attempting to catch a fly ball and received serious injuries.

Scott based his lawsuit against the college on the fact that the school officials should have foreseen the possibility that a player, during a game, would forget abut the flag pole's location and run into it. He argued that this constituted a hazard that reasonably prudent people would have removed.

The New York Court supported his charges and held the defendant liable for Scott's injuries by awarding him $12,000.

Thomas Healy was an infant of 3½ years who wandered from his mother who was in the restroom of the gymnasium.[17] He went into the locker room next to the restroom and pulled on the lockers which were not attached to the wall. The lockers fell on his head and he sustained injuries.

The officials of Georgetown College appealed an earlier decision in behalf of the young boy but the higher court also agreed with the previous ruling. It felt that the condition of the lockers caused the injury and supported the plaintiff's claim of negligence.

A higher court of appeals reversed a decision that awarded $45,000 to a man injured at a football game.[18] Maurice Richards attended a Thanksgiving Day game in Michigan and was injured when the bleachers collapsed. Richards contended that the school owed the spectators the standard of care necessary to protect them from injury. He claimed that the school did not inspect the bleachers or put them up correctly.

The Appellate Court felt that the bleachers fell because enthusiastic fans were swaying and causing the bleachers to be thrown against each other. It therefore disallowed the award and ruled in favor of the school district.

A question concerning governmental immunity was at stake in Michigan when Nancy Cody fell from a mini-trampoline and broke her arms.[19] Nancy's father sued the physical education teacher for forcing her to participate against her will, and the principal for delaying medical treatment.

The school district answered the claim by stating that they were "pursuing a governmental function and thereby not liable for the injury." Michigan courts have held that school districts enjoy immunity for their negligent acts. The plaintiff did not agree because he charged that the physical education class was a proprietary function engaged in by the school district.

The court then relied on *Richards v. Birmingham School District* in which bleachers collapsed. The court held that despite the profit-making nature of the contest, football was still under the physical education program of the school and denied recovery by the injured man.

The next question concerned the allegation that the defective condition of the building contributed to the plaintiff's injuries. Michigan had permitted suits for injuries that were the result of the poor condition of a public building. The court did not accept this claim either, since the mini-trampoline was merely an object in a building and did not qualify as an exception.

The court then answered a final contention that

the school district purchased liability insurance and
therefore waived its immunity. The plaintiff
charged that the purchase of liability insurance
should constitute such a waiver or "governmental
agencies are wasting a great deal of money
protecting against risks which do not exist."

The Appeals Court of Michigan answered this
argument by saying that a school district needed
such insurance as protection against the "areas
where the legislature had eliminated their immunity
. . . injuries resulting from motor vehicles accidents
and defective buildings."

It responded to all the charges by ruling that the
doctrine of governmental immunity was upheld.

Medical Treatment and Excuses

Although teachers are not expected to be
physicians, coaches and physical education
teachers are expected to administer life-saving
first aid when needed. But this is where the court
says stop! There is a temptation on the part of
coaches and physical education teachers to
suggest remedies and go beyond emergency first
aid. The law does not expect, require, or even
want such conduct. In many situations the lack of
action or wrong action can result in a law suit
that possibly could have been avoided.

Judith Lowe had three notes from her doctor in
which he supported her claim of a physical
disability due to a previous injury.[20] Her physical
education teacher ignored the notes and Judith's

protest and directed her to participate in an activity known as the broad jump.

Judith contended that she was injured because the teacher disregarded her excuses and made her engage in such a vigorous activity.

At the trial, Judith failed to produce medical testimony to support her claim. The Appellate Court therefore ordered a new trial in which both liability and damages would be considered.

Edwin Quinn was accidently kicked during an activity in his physical education class.[21] The accident occurred near 1:00 p.m. and he became very dizzy but did not lose consciousness. About an hour later he left with a friend and went to his family doctor. His doctor sent him to the hospital about 3:00 p.m.

Edwin was x-rayed at the hospital but the x-rays failed to reveal the blood clot or fracture he received. Later the boy died and the doctor observed that an earlier diagnosis and subsequent surgery could have saved his life.

At the time Edwin was examined at school, it was reported that his eyes appeared normal and did not indicate the later symptoms of serious brain damage.

The court did not uphold the claim against the school of negligence due to delay in treatment. It reversed the earlier decision instead and favored the school.

Robert Mogabgab was running sprints near the close of football practice in Louisiana.[22] On the way to the team bus, he fell from exhaustion and began vomiting. The bus arrived at the high school from the field about twenty minutes later and his teammates placed him on the floor of the cafeteria. Later they took him to the shower and placed him on a blanket.

At this time, one of his coaches became concerned about his condition and put an ammonia capsule by his nose. He then brought a first aid manual into the cafeteria and the coaches discussed the clamminess of his skin and his heavy breathing. The coaches talked about his condition and possible treatment.

Later a parent of a fellow player came to pick up her son and saw the boy on the floor. She told her husband that Robert needed immediate treatment but that the coach had previously refused to call a doctor.

Robert's mother was called and she in turn called her doctor who sent Robert to the Southern Baptist Hospital where his condition was described as "profound heat exhaustion and shock to an advanced degree, but not necessarily irreversible."

Robert died the following day and his parents sued for damages because they felt that their son's death was due to the unnecessary delay in getting him medical attention.

The defendants testified that the parents knew that Robert had blood pressure and abnormal heart problems. They accused the parents of permitting Robert to assume the risk of playing football and charged that they were, in fact, guilty of contributory negligence.

The trial court dismissed the case and it was appealed. The higher court ruled that the coaches erred in denying Robert proper medical treatment by attempting to administer first aid in an untrained manner. The court remarked that the plaintiffs presented sufficient evidence to substantiate their charge that their son died because he did not see a doctor until it was too late to save his life.

It awarded damages to each parent of $20,000, medical costs of $639.50 and funeral expenses of $941.25.

IN MY OPINION

Injuries mean various things to many people; sort of different strokes for different folks. To the coach an injury means the loss of a good player, perhaps the difference between victory and defeat. To the administrator it can mean unexpected doctor bills, ambulance costs and other unforeseen costs that were not budgeted. To the parent it can mean additional expenses that were not foreseen because most parents believe that their daughters and sons are protected by school insurance. Frequently this is not the case and confidence is lost between both parents and school officials.

The costs of injuries are reaching record proportions and lawsuits are resulting in awards that stagger one's imagination.

The source of most injury litigation in physical
education and athletics comes about by alleged lack
of supervision. The court is very tolerant and does
not expect the impossible but it does require
reasonable conduct from a supervisor. It wants
teachers and coaches to look ahead at what can
happen and then use the care a reasonable person
would use. Teachers who use equipment that is
dangerous, such as trampolines, spring boards,
gymnastic equipment and the like, are expected to
remain in the immediate area where students are
using or likely to use such apparatus.

It is sound policy to keep a facility such as a
gymnasium closed unless supervision can be
provided. Again, however, the court does not require
that playgrounds and gymnasiums be supervised on
holidays or after school hours. In the past the court
has reasoned that these areas are safer for students
than busy, traffic-laden streets. The court draws the
line when school authorities permit their facilities to
be open when defective conditions or equipments
exist. In these instances, it is better to close the
facility until the unsafe condition is remedied. If a
gymnasium is open and rough or rowdy play is
known to school officials, then the area should be
supervised or closed.

When accidents occur that could have taken place
even with supervision, there seems to be little
chance of liability against the school.

The court does not hold colleges or high schools
responsible for intramural or after school activities

if the activities are relatively safe and the facilities are not defective.

Governmental immunity still receives tremendous opposition by people everywhere, but in fact, remains strongly entrenched as a means of defense for states and their school districts. If a trend is evolving it would appear to be dissatisfaction to the point of future change by many states. Many court decisions have interesting and often prophetic dicta by judges. Several years later the dissent becomes the guiding power as judicial trends become reality. Possibly the opposition to governmental immunity in recent cases will manifest itself in new policy in the days ahead. There appears to be little doubt that teachers will not be cloaked in immunity. For this reason, teachers and coaches must accept their responsibilities and be aware and alert to the problems of liability.

Teachers and coaches must realize the importance of medical treatment. Handle emergencies, but do not try to treat as a physician. Keep in close contact at all times with a doctor about the advisability of using a player who has been injured by returning him to practice or games. Do not make students participate when doctors provide medical excuses. *Be safe rather than sorry.* As coaches and physical education teachers, know the rudiments of first aid, don't gamble that accidents will not happen to you.

The wise teacher and coach will take precautions, warn students of inherent dangers involved in the activities and facilities, act prudently and then go about their job with confidence. Fear should not cause activities that are educationally sound to be eliminated. A knowledge of what can and should be done, realizing that injuries are inevitable and not all involve litigation, should help ease the mind of all.

1. Dailey v. Los Angeles Unified School Dist., 470 P.2d 360 (Cal. 1970).
2. Segerman v. Jones, 259 A.2d 794 (Md. 1969).
3. *Id.*
4. *Id.*
5. Lueck v. City of Janesville, 204 N.W.2d 6 (Wis. 1973).
6. Armlin v. Board of Educ. of Middleburgh Central School Dist., 320 N.Y.S.2d 402 (1971).
7. Albers v. Independent School Dist. No. 302, 487 P.2d 936 (Idaho 1971).
8. Kaufman v. City of N.Y., 214 N.Y.S.2d 767 (1961).
9. Frazier v. YMCA of Little Falls, 144 N.Y.S.2d 448 (1955).
10. Rubtchinsky v. State Univ. of N.Y. at Albany, 260 N.Y.S.2d 256 (1965).
11. Morehouse College v. Russell, 136 S.E.2d 179 (Ga. 1964).
12. Driscol v. Delphi Community School Corp., 290 N.E.2d 769 (Ind. 1972).
13. Bush v. Smith, 289 N.E.2d 800 (Ind. 1972).
14. Darrow v. West Genesee Central School Dist., 342 N.Y.S.2d 611 (1973).
15. Stanley v. Board of Educ. of City of Chicago, 293 N.E.2d 417 (Ill. 1973).
16. Scott v. State, 158 N.Y.S.2d 617 (1956).
17. President & Directors of Georgetown College v. Healy, 244 F.2d 785 (D.C. Cir. 1957).
18. Richards v. School Dist. of City of Birmingham, 83 N.W.2d 643 (Mich. 1957).
19. Cody v. Southfield-Lathrup School Dist., 181 N.W.2d 81 (Mich. 1970).
20. Lowe v. Board of Educ. of City of N.Y., 321 N.Y.S.2d 508 (1971).

21. Peck v. Board of Educ. of City of Mt. Vernon, 317 N.Y.S.2d 919 (1970).
22. Mogabgab v. Orleans Parish School Bd., 239 So. 2d 456 (La. App. 1970).

10. Athletics— A Right or Privilege

*We just feel athletes should have the
same rights as other students.*[1]

Due process, or the right of an individual to receive fair play, has been extolled by coaches for years. Simply stated, the Bill of Rights promises each person the opportunity to be a first class citizen. Specifically, the Fifth Amendment of the United States Constitution states that "No person ... shall be deprived of life, liberty, or property without due process of law." The Fifth Amendment applies only to the federal government. The Fourteenth Amendment, however, extends this concept to cover the operations of state governments as well, in reading, "nor shall any State deprive any person of life, liberty, or property without due process of law."

The Supreme Court historically has refused to define due process, preferring instead to consider it a "gradual process of judicial inclusion and exclusion." [2] The law distinguishes between due process as substantive and as procedural.

Substantive due process protects each person by requiring that a state must have a valid goal before it can deprive an individual of his right to life, liberty, or property. To take one example, children may be required to have a vaccination to protect them from disease before attending school. The vaccination is, in this instance, employed to insure the objective of the state and meets the requirement of substantial due process.[3]

Procedural due process includes the following conditions:

1. an individual must have proper notice that he is about to be deprived of life, liberty, or property;
2. an individual must be given the opportunity to be heard; and
3. an individual must be afforded a fair trial or hearing.[4]

Not all due process rights have been accorded all educational institutions. A distinction has developed between public and private institutions because of the application and interpretation of the Fourteenth Amendment.[5] If an educational institution is classified as private, its students have no constitutional protections under the Fourteenth Amendment. Instead, the courts rely on a contract theory, as decided in *Dixon v. Alabama State Board of Education*,[6] to safeguard the right of private school students to the protection afforded by due process. Under this contract theory an agreement is presumed to exist which provides that an institution

will not act in an arbitrary manner toward its
students in disciplinary cases.

Due process rights are guaranteed to students who
attend public schools under the Fourteenth
Amendment. While the courts have traditionally
supported the authority of school officials to set
rules and maintain order, it does insist on rules that
are reasonable.[7]

Today, more and more questions are being raised
that require consideration of due process.

1. Should athletics be classified as a right
   or a privilege?
2. Should an institution be penalized for
   the illegal action of a coach or athlete?
3. Should all sports in a college program be
   penalized for the illegal action of staff
   or participants in one sport, such as
   basketball?
4. Should coaches and athletes be subjected
   to signed statements and polygraph
   tests to prove their allegiance to
   institutional and association rules?

It is apparent that these and other controversies
over rights in athletics will continue until some
definitive action is taken by the courts. There are
some who consider athletics to be purely voluntary
and extracurricular. To them athletics represents a
privilege and therefore is not subject to governance
by law. On the other hand, there are those who
argue that athletics is curricular in nature and
therefore is protected by law.

The courts take opposing views on the issue. One

reported that "varsity sports, unlike intramurals, are a discretionary privilege and not a property right." [8] Another agreed and classified athletics as a "privilege which may be claimed only in accordance with the standards set up for participation." [9] But an Indiana court stated that athletics are a right and therefore that participants enjoy equal protection under the Fourteenth Amendment.[10]

The Commissioner of Education in New Jersey put athletics in the area of rights when he ruled on a controversial hairstyle case.[11] The Commissioner warned coaches that although they have the obligation to select members of a team based on ability, they could not deny a student the opportunity to try out for a team because of a particular hairstyle.

The courts, however, confuse the already cloudy issue by commenting that:

> it [athletics] remains a privilege founded upon a right to participate in what admittedly are activities forming an integral part of the school curriculum.[12]

and in another instance, that:

> the privilege of interscholastic competition is outside the protection of due process and a student is not given a federally "constitutional right" to participate in a sport unless his rights under the equal protection clause are violated.[13]

A sampling of decisions may offer insight into the attitude of the courts toward the rights of athletes and coaches.

Alleged Violation of the Rights of Athletes

Cecil New Jr. was, allegedly, permanently injured and paralyzed from the neck down as the result of an injury received while he was playing football at the University of Kentucky.[14] New pointed out that the athletic department used athletes like him to obtain athletic prestige, satisfy the egos of old grads and secure revenue through gate receipts and television. He charged the Kentucky Athletic Association with minimizing the physical and emotional dangers to the athletes who accept the offer to play without "question, challenge, inspection, or investigation."

New sued the University for allowing the athletic department to improperly coach him in the correct technique of tackling and the failure to provide him with a safe head-gear. He testified that the University failed to honor an oral promise it made him after his injury. New stated that he was promised:

(1) complete college education, books, personal attendants, transportation;
(2) complete medical and hospital care for life including services of physicians and surgeons with all special appliances;
(3) a home suitably equipped and furnished to take care of his needs;
(4) an automobile suited for his condition;
(5) financial assistance and aid as might be necessary to live reasonably for the rest of his life.

He charged the defendants with breach of contract on all but part 1 and 2.

New then added a charge unexpected in cases like this when he claimed that his rights as a citizen of Ohio were deprived because of his injury.

The NCAA vehemently responded that it could understand a lawsuit for personal injuries from a tort, a breach of contract or even a products liability case, but in no sense could it be a *civil rights case.*

The plaintiff's case was denied as the court based its denial for the $10 million on the immunity protecting the University by the Eleventh Amendment.

The Eleventh Amendment reads:

> the Judicial power of the United States shall not be construed to extend to any suit in law or equity, commenced or prosecuted against one of the United States by Citizens of another State, or by Citizens or Subjects of any Foreign State.

While the plaintiff lost his case, this new dimension involving alleged deprivation of rights may be the start of a future trend.

Eligibility Cases

Robert Parish, a 7' 1" basketball player, was described as a "super athlete" in the mold of Wilt Chamberlain and Abdul-Jabbar. *Basketball News* chose him as the top basketball player in the United States and he was named to several All American Teams.[15]

Centenary College recruited Parish and when this became known, an NCAA official called the basketball coach to inquire about Parish's ability to predict the 1.600 average necessary to play.

The coach replied that Parish would take the ACT test and convert the score to meet the requirement. Parish actually took the ACT test twice in an attempt to qualify for admission. It was said that Parish had been deprived both "educationally and economically" and that when the "baskets began to swish" he attempted to prepare himself academically in the hope of obtaining a scholarship.

Until 1969 the NCAA permitted institutions the opportunity to adopt their own standards and policy by developing its own tables with which students could be measured. An institution could use the national tables or adopt a conference set of tables. The NCAA also permitted an institution to allow prospective students the choice of the ACT or SAT test.

As of May 1, 1970 all NCAA member institutions were advised that they could no longer convert the ACT test score to the SAT.

The NCAA's 1.600 Rule stated that a member of the NCAA could not practice or play the freshman year any individual who did not predict a 1.600.

Some NCAA members chose not to follow the 1.600 Rule which denied them post season competition.

Centenary College, however, elected to adhere to the 1.600 Rule. When the basketball coach was informed of the change in ACT test scores he ignored the NCAA's warning. Although the officials of Centenary College were aware of the Rule and forewarned by the NCAA officials, they attempted to obtain an injunction against the NCAA to prevent the enforcement of the 1.600 Rule. Centenary argued that the 1.600 Rule was unconstitutional under the Fourteenth Amendment.

The NCAA put the burden on Centenary College to declare Parish ineligible but the officials of the College refused to take such action.

Centenary College contended that Parish was from a small rural school and a poor background. It felt that the SAT and ACT were discriminatory in nature toward black students.

The NCAA pointed out that the 1.600 Rule was adopted in an attempt to protect poor risk students from exploitation. The Rule was also an attempt to set standards to be more compatible with other schools.

The Court supported the argument of the NCAA and also commented on the claim that Parish was the victim of discrimination by referring to *Murray v. West Baton Rouge School Bd.*[16] when it was said that:

> if a few black students whose educational progress has been wrongly retarded because of this testing; it is most unfortunate. The fact that the tests might not be valid for a few students does not constitute deprivation. Members of the black race have been perhaps the greatest

beneficiaries of numerically disproportionate participation in intercollegiate athletics and they have done so under the 1.600 Rule.

The Court favored the NCAA and denied the requested injunction.

Junior College Transfer Sues ECAC

Norman Bounds was a basketball player at the State University of New York on Brockport's team until the school declared him ineligible.[17]

Bounds sued the ECAC because it had a rule that a junior college transfer had to have 48 hours of transferable credit to be eligible for athletic participation. He had 58 hours from Erie Community College but Brockport only accepted 34 hours. Bounds then attended summer school and gained 18 hours credit but Erie Community College refused to accept the 18 hours and put it on his transcript.

The Court dismissed the case and listed its reasons for such action:

1. Brockport, not the ECAC, declared Bounds ineligible and he did not take action against the University.
2. The ECAC has no power against the individual, just the school.
3. If the plaintiff felt that his rights had been violated he could seek relief against Brockport.
4. There is no proof that the ECAC has threatened any action against

Brockport which would impair the plaintiff's rights.

5. If the plaintiff establishes his right to play by action against Brockport and then the ECAC steps in, then, action can be considered against them.

Regular Season Champion Denied Playoff Berth

Fisk University's basketball team won the regular Southern Intercollegiate Athletic Conference play and established themselves as the NCAA representatives.[18]

The basketball coach at Alabama State University sent a letter to the SIAC Commissioner and charged that George House and William Sweatt were ineligible.

Fisk University's representatives met with Conference officials and were advised that their team could participate in the SIAC Tournament. No action was to be taken until after the Tournament.

On the day of the Tournament, in fact, five minutes before Fisk played, the President of the Conference told the Fisk coach that Sweatt could not play because of the protest. The President's rule superseded the Commissioner and Fisk was defeated by Morehouse College, 77-74, and eliminated from the Tournament.

Without an explanation, Fisk University was notified that they could not compete in the NCAA Playoffs.

Fisk University took the case to court arguing that the action had caused injury and irreparable harm to the University. They sought an injunction which would compel the NCAA to allow Fisk University to compete in the Playoffs until the issue was settled.

The Chancery Court of Tennessee did not feel that Fisk University had the right to represent the Conference. It ruled that the University did play an ineligible player and as a result must forfeit all SIAC games and be denied the regular season championship and NCAA representation in the playoffs.

"Extra Event" Causes Ineligibility

Frederick Samara was a senior at the University of Pennsylvania. He received an invitation to compete in the Russian-American Indoor Track Meet in Richmond, Virginia, in March, 1973.[19]

Under NCAA regulations, this event qualified as an "Extra Event" and required certification by the sponsoring organization, the Amateur Athletic Union. If the event was not certified, the NCAA rule stated that:

> he shall be denied eligibility for intercollegiate track and field competition, if, while a candidate for the intercollegiate team in track and field, he participates in track and field competition which is subject to the certification program sponsored by BYLAW 2 but which has not been certified.

The AAU did not request certification which the NCAA would have granted.

Samara sought an injunction against the NCAA to prevent it from taking any disciplinary action for his participation in the track meet. He claimed that the action of the NCAA violated his rights under the First, Fifth, and Fourteenth Amendments.

The Court responded that the requirement of certification designed to limit abuses was reasonable. It observed that if the NCAA had denied the AAU's application for certification, a valid issue would be at stake. Since the AAU did not seek certification the court found no violation of any right and dismissed the case.

Isaac Curtis was admitted to the University of California at Berkeley under a special program known as the "four percent rule." [20] Students could be admitted without SAT or ACT test scores or other admission procedures. The only criterion was the individual's potential for academic success.

The University discovered that Curtis did not predict a 1.600 average when he entered. He testified that he was unaware of the need for any test to establish athletic eligibility. The University officials explained that Curtis was not advised of the test requirement due to a clerical error. The NCAA was notified and although Curtis had a B+ average at the time, declared him ineligible. In addition the NCAA revoked the points he scored in the NCAA Championship Track and Field Meet and ruled that he was ineligible for one additional year following the freshman year.

The University refused to accept the NCAA's ruling and would not declare Curtis ineligible.

The NCAA then imposed sanctions against the

University and declared that six other athletes illegally received financial aid and were not certified for competition.

Unlike the previous cases listed above, the court upheld Curtis's contention that his rights were violated. It also found the 1.600 Rule unconstitutional and not applicable since Curtis was in good academic standing. It prohibited the NCAA from enforcing the 1.600 Rule's penalty against Curtis and the sanctions against the University.

The NCAA has appealed the decision and it will be interesting to follow the progress of the case as the higher court reviews the testimony. The decision may be reversed as it was in *Associated Students v. NCAA*, discussed in Chapter 7,[21] or it may be affirmed and thereby strike a serious blow to the NCAA.

The NCAA discarded the 1.600 Rule and went to a different standard for eligibility. Instead of a predicted average based on class rank and SAT scores, the NCAA adopted a 2.00 Rule which in reality is a "C" average for a high school graduate. The 2.00 average is generally considered an easier requirement than the old 1.600 Rule.

2.00 Rule Challenged in Court

Paul Schubert was an outstanding tennis player who wanted to attend Ball State University.[22] The NCAA's 1.600 Rule was replaced by a 2.00 Rule which Ball State accepted. The officials of Ball State notified Schubert that he did not have a 2.00 average and could not practice or play on the tennis team during his freshman year.

Schubert sought judicial relief from Ball State and from the ruling of the NCAA, claiming his rights as protected by the First, Ninth, and Fourteenth Amendments.

The Appellate Court referred to *San Antonio v. Rodriguez* [23] in which the U. S. Supreme Court ruled that there is no constitutional right to an education. It reasoned, therefore, that in like manner, there could be no constitutional right to participate in intercollegiate athletics.

Schubert argued that he had passed two quarters of academic work and, since he had given this evidence of academic ability, that the 2.00 Rule was unconstitutional in denying him the right to participate in spring sports. He also pointed out that some NCAA member schools did not elect to be governed by the 2.00 Rule and that Ball State did not have the right to adopt the rule.

The court, by dismissing the case, supported Ball State, deciding that it lacked evidence that the academic performance of a college student in his freshman year predicted success in college more accurately than high school grades. It warned that such a practice, if adopted, would encourage some coaches to recruit less academically able students who possessed outstanding athletic skills in the hope that they could obtain satisfactory first semester grades and be eligible for the second semester.

The court concluded by strongly asserting that

Ball State had the right to adopt the 2.00 Rule, just as it was not required to offer a course in nuclear physics simply because other schools included it in their curriculum.

Foreign Students

NCAA officials have reportedly admitted that their regulations regarding foreign students is the only area in which they have been defeated in court. The attitude of the courts is reflected in two cases that concern foreign students who participated in American inter-collegiate athletics.

Two Canadian nationals were recruited by Boston University to play ice hockey.[24] The two sued the ECAC and NCAA, which had declared them ineligible, in the hope that they could be ruled eligible and thereby that the Associations would be prevented from imposing sanctions on Boston University.

The point at issue involved expense money paid to these students to play Major Junior A Team hockey in Canada. William Buckton moved to a town to play Major Junior A Team hockey and received $24.00 per week for his room and board, $10.00 per week for expenses and $4.82 for books. Another plaintiff referred to as Marzo also played in a town where he received similar expenses.

In Canada, schools do not sponsor ice hockey and students must rely on civic or recreation programs to furnish competition. At times, outstanding athletes leave home and attend schools in towns where the level of competition, such as that provided by the Major Junior A Team, is available. Teams openly and legitimately pay for the expenses of such athletes.

The two players argued that the ECAC and NCAA did not specify prior to 1971 that players who participated in Major Junior A Hockey would be ineligible for participation at American colleges. As soon as the rule was passed, Buckton and Marzo withdrew from the Major Junior A competition.

The athletes argued that a friend of theirs from Canada played for a preparatory school in the United States and received more financial aid than they did in Canada. They testified that they could see no difference in the two situations. Their friend, however, was eligible for collegiate play while they were not.

Although the NCAA responded to the charges by stressing the fact that the rule was designed to protect "amateurism" in sports, the court found it suspect. The court felt that the rule set different standards for Canadians than for those who played in the United States. The court also deplored the stigma that ineligibility places on a student-athlete and felt that the penalty would cause "serious and irreparable harm" to the two athletes.

The court ordered the officials of Boston University to refrain from action that would cause the two players to be ineligible. It then directed the NCAA to withhold all sanctions against Boston University until the case was decided.

Howard University finished third in the NCAA Soccer Championships in 1970 and won it in 1971.[25] Several schools reported that Howard University had played an ineligible player in 1970 and four players in 1971 and demanded punitive action against the athletes and the University.

After a thorough investigation, the NCAA prohibited Howard University from qualifying in the 1973 tournament and directed it to return all 1970 and 1971 trophies. Howard University and the athletes in question sued the NCAA on the basis of the Fourteenth Amendment's equal protection clause. The plaintiffs charged that the right of due process had been denied them and they attacked three NCAA regulations during the trial:

1) the five-year Rule
2) the 1.600 Rule
3) the foreign-student Rule

The court considered the five-year Rule which requires a student athlete to complete four years of participation within a five year period. Since the rule applies to all students, foreign and American alike, in the same manner, the court saw no discrimination in it.

The 1.600 Rule applies only to post season events. While this rule was designed to eliminate the exploitation of athletes and may pose some difficulties to foreign students, it was not considered unfair by the court.

The rule causing foreign students to lose one year of eligibility for every year after their nineteenth

birthday was a different story. The Court supported
the plaintiff's argument that the rule did not apply
to American athletes and was arbitrary,
unreasonable, vague and definitely advantageous to
American athletes.

The Court took exception to the charge that due
process was violated. It reported that Howard
University and Mori Diane, one of the athletes
involved, were given the opportunity for a hearing
but did not request one.

The Court concluded, however, that the NCAA's
foreign student rule did represent a violation of the
equal protection clause and as such enjoined it from
imposing any penalty on Howard University or its
soccer players, based on this specific regulation.

Rights of Coaches

At the NCAA's 69th Annual Convention in
January, 1975, various topics were discussed but
priority was given to the area of rights.[26]

Dr. Stephen Horn, the president of California
State University at Long Beach, proposed legislation
that would penalize coaches involved in misconduct,
who cause their institutions to be placed on
probation. Horn, whose institution suffered NCAA
sanctions, requested the NCAA to prevent guilty
coaches from moving to member schools until the
probationary period was over. His proposal passed
easily.

At the same time, the NCAA members passed
additional legislation to compel every athlete and

coach to certify each year that they have obeyed the rules of their institution and the NCAA. The Southwest Conference has gone even further and adopted a policy that might become national procedure in a short time. When complaints of illegal recruitment and other rule violations are made, athletes and coaches involved will be subjected to a polygraph test. While there is no court case on record to offer a precedent, it is possible that this rule may soon be tested in court.

Seton Hall University may have become the first institution to penalize staff members for alleged recruiting violations. Following the January 1975 NCAA Convention, President Msgr. Thomas Fahy, in the same month, announced the following action taken by the University:

1. declared sophomore Glenn Mosley ineligible for further basketball competition because he played during his freshman year and did not qualify under the NCAA rule requiring a "C" average in high school;
2. suspended his athletic director for three weeks, his head basketball coach for one month and the assistant coach for two weeks;
3. fined the athletic director $500, the head coach $650 and the assistant coach $100.

President Fahy stated that the University took the action. The NCAA has been investigating the alleged violation and has not taken action at this time. Fahy made it clear that the University might institute a lawsuit to challenge the NCAA's 2.00 Rule in an attempt to regain Mosley's eligibility.

The suspensions by Seton Hall represent immediate action following the "get tough" proposal of Stephen Horn of Long Beach and may indicate the greater involvement of college presidents in the athletic programs at their institutions.[27]

While there is much concern over the conduct of coaches regarding illegal practices, an interesting case illustrates the action a court took regarding the dismissal of a teacher from his position as basketball coach.

Roger Furman coached basketball, was sponsor for the Student Council, and taught classes at Comanche High School in Iowa.[28] Furman suspended several players before an important game and his team suffered an embarrassing loss. After the game, he told a reporter that he was sorry he took so long to get the "riff-raff" off the team.

Furman's critical remarks created an unfavorable reaction in the community and his principal and athletic director asked him to resign. He refused, but at the school board's next meeting was relieved of his duties as basketball coach for the following season. The school board retained him, however, as a teacher and as sponsor of the Student Council.

Furman requested and was granted a hearing before the school board but to no avail, since it reaffirmed its earlier decision. When notified, Furman disputed the board's procedure, arguing that he was not given proper notice of the charges against him.

The Iowa District Court agreed that the initial hearing was held before the coach could plead his case and ruled that the belated hearing did "not provide an important tribunal and was a violation of [Furman's] rights to due process of law."

It declared that since Furman had been illegally discharged as basketball coach, he was reinstated for the following year. The Court stated that he was employed under contract and that this could not be modified or any part of it terminated by the board.

IN MY OPINION

For the first time since 1736 a California court ruled that a prisoner might, under certain conditions, have the right to escape from jail.[29] The case resulted from the escape of two female prisoners from a narcotics rehabilitation center and attracted nationwide publicity. The two women claimed that a group of lesbians threatened them with physical harm if they refused to engage in sex acts.

Three days later, the United States Supreme Court decided that pupils have a Constitutional right to know why they are being suspended and, in turn, have the right to a hearing.[30] The hearing may be simply a meeting between the pupil and the disciplinarian.

It is obvious that the issue of civil rights in all areas, including athletics, is being recognized increasingly by the courts.

For one reason or another, many people associated

with athletics become irritated when student rights
are mentioned. It may be due to past memories of
student riots, barricaded doors, and the takeover of
facilities. Whatever the memories are, the fact
remains that athletics in the seventies will be
subjected to much litigation involving questions of
due process.

I learned about due process, or the lack of it, the
hard way. Our basketball team was on an extended
winning streak and appeared ready to defend the
national NAIA title won in Kansas City the previous
year. I was jolted from complacency by the
unpleasant realization that our team was under
investigation. A source who requested that he
remain anonymous reported that several coaches
were diligently working behind the scenes to prove
that one of our players had transferred from another
school and was ineligible.

It appeared that if the allegation was true, our
record would drop from the top to the bottom and we
would lose the opportunity to defend our title. Our
school would receive unfavorable publicity as our
basketball recruiting would be ridiculed. Most
important of all, our young freshman would be ruled
permanently ineligible for his four years in college.
What a price to pay!

After twenty days of rumor, innuendo,
unfavorable publicity and a total lack of due process,
we were notified that, after a thorough
investigation, we were innocent of the charges.

I could not help wonder how often coaches,

athletes and institutions have been put through a similar situation without the benefit of due process.

A new trend may be developing on college campuses as athletes seek the same rights as other students. Kathy Kidd, the student body president at Oklahoma University, exemplified this new attitude.[31] Kathy has openly challenged the athletic department's regulations as inconsistent with those enjoyed by the student body. She charged that the athletic department limited hours for female visitation in the athletic dormitory, placed restrictions on food, beer and television in the rooms, and questioned the right of access by the department to the rooms of the athletes.

The Student Court at Oklahoma University supported her allegations and ruled that the rules imposed on the athletes violated the U. S. Bill of Rights and added that the right of privacy was *absolute*.

The Oklahoma controversy may or may not be indicative of a new direction toward athletes and rights but one thing appears certain; that the U. S. Constitution and its established guidelines will seek safeguards through the courts to protect their rights as never before.

1. Greensboro Daily News, December 26, 1974.
2. Davidson v. New Orleans, 96 U.S. 97 (1887).
3. K. Alexander, R. Corns, W. McCann, Public School Law, West Publishing Co., St. Paul, Minn. 1969.
4. *Id.*
5. *1972-1973 Annual Survey of American Law*, New York University.

6. Dixon v. Alabama State Bd. of Educ., 294 F.2d 150 (5th Cir. 1961).

7. *1972-1973 Annual Survey of American Law, supra* note 5.

8. *Nolpe Notes*, National Organization of Legal Problems of Education, Vol. 7, No. 4, April, 1972.

9. Kissick v. Garland Independent School Dist., 330 S.W.2d 708 (Tex. 1959).

10. Wellsand v. Valparaiso Community School Corp., Case No. 71H 122 (2) (USDC Ind. 1971).

11. Harriss v. Teaneck Bd. of Educ., Decision of New Jersey Commissioner of Education (1970).

12. Brown v. Wells, 181 N.W.2d 708 (Minn. 1970).

13. Wellsand v. Valparaiso, *supra* note 10.

14. New v. University of Kentucky & NCAA, USDC #8077 (Ohio 1973).

15. Parish v. NCAA, 361 F. Supp. 1220 (La. 1973).

16. Murray v. West Baton Rouge Parish School Bd., 472 F.2d 438 (5th Cir. 1973).

17. Bounds v. Eastern College Athletic Conference, N.Y. Supreme Court (1972).

18. Fisk University v. Southern Intercollegiate Athletic Conference, Davidson County Chancery Court, No. A-2309-A (Tenn. 1973).

19. Samara v. NCAA, USDC No. 104-72-A (Va. 1973).

20. Curtis v. NCAA, USDC No. C71-2088 ACW (Cal. 1972).

21. Associated Students, Inc. of California State Univ. v. NCAA, Civil No. S-2754 (Cal. 1973).

22. Schubert v. NCAA & Ball State Univ., U.S. Ct. of Appeals No. 74-1282 (Ind. 1974).

23. San Antonio Ind. School Dist. v. Rodriguez, 411 U.S. 1 (1973).

24. Buckton v. NCAA, 366 F. Supp. 1152 (Mass. 1973).

25. Howard University v. NCAA, 367 F. Supp. 926 (D.C. 1973).
26. Greensboro Daily News, January 9, 1975.
27. Greensboro Daily News, January 31, 1975.
28. Board of Directors of Comanche School Dist. v. Furman, Dist. Ct. No. CL582-0674 (Iowa 1974).
29. Greensboro Daily News, January 20, 1975.
30. Greensboro Daily News, January 23, 1975.
31. Greensboro Daily News, December 26, 1974.

11. The Final Whistle

Participation in athletics and physical education activities has reached an all-time high in the 1970's. In like manner, litigation involving athletic activities has increased to record proportions. Damage awards have grown accordingly and large awards are not the exception today, but more likely the rule. Courts are reluctant to reduce awards due to the decreasing value of the dollar or perhaps a new attitude toward the individual who receives such an award.

Lawsuits involving athletics will continue to flood the court dockets as people are more knowledgeable of their legal remedies and individual rights. It is apparent that athletics and law have entered a new era.

Administrators, coaches, and teachers question their lines of authority over litigation that confronts them. Civil rights cases continue to plague schoolmen as litigants charge that their constitutional rights are violated in many school-related law suits.

It appears that the court would prefer to return considerable authority to state and local regulatory bodies. It will not tolerate, however, rules and regulations that are arbitrary, capricious, or unreasonable. The key word in athletic litigation seems to be *reasonable*! The court expects and even demands action by school officials that exemplifies reasonable conduct, action and judgment.

The court has made it clear that not every rule that is challenged nor injury that is sustained will result in a lawsuit or unfavorable decision to coaches and teachers. It consistently upholds school people whenever they act in good faith and use sound judgment. It will not tolerate outmoded rules, grossly negligent conduct and arbitrary regulations by those who are in positions of authority. The court has shifted the emphasis to the welfare of the individual rather than the school and this represents a dramatic change.

The court will not permit a double standard to exist regarding race, creed, color or sex in athletics.

New state and federal legislation, while bitterly opposed at many levels, will be proposed more than ever in the days ahead. Safety and health legislation will continue to be an issue as legislators seek to curb the ills and dangers that frequently exist in sports today.

Although litigation frustrates administrators, coaches, teachers, and athletes alike, such litigation and the subsequent exposure to the public eye should prove beneficial to athletics as a whole.

Athletics can survive such exposure and create conditions that will make it safer to all concerned and, in reality, what educators, spectators and participants want it to be.

Athletics and the law truly represent a "whole new ballgame" but one that should be the best ever.

TABLE OF CASES

State v. Greenwald, 265 A.2d 720 (Conn. 1969), Ch. 2, n. 9.

State v. Stevenson, 189 N.E.2d 181 (Ohio 1962), Ch. 3, n. 22.

Stevenson v. Wheeler County Bd. of Educ., 306 F. Supp. 97 (S.D. Ga. 1969), Ch. 3, n. 19.

Stringer v. Gould, 314 N.Y.S.2d 309 (1970), Ch. 8, n. 9.

Sturrup v. Mahan, 290 N.E.2d 64 (Ind. 1972), Ch. 6, n. 15.

Taylor v. Wake Forest Univ., 191 S.E.2d 379 (N.C. 1972), Ch. 7, n. 4.

Tinker v. Des Moines Independent Community School Dist., 393 U.S. 503 (1969), Ch. 2, nn. 14, 15.

Truitt v. Gaines, 318 F.2d 461 (3d Cir. 1963), Ch. 4, nn. 32, 34.

Wellsand v. Valparaiso Community School Corp., Case No. 71 H 122 (2) (U.S.D.C. Ind. 1971), Ch. 3, n. 24; Ch. 10, nn. 10, 13.

Williams v. Eaton, 443 F.2d 422 (10th Cir. 1971), Ch. 2, n. 19.

Zanders v. Louisiana State Bd. of Educ., 281 F. Supp. 747 (W.D. La. 1968), Ch. 2, n. 8.

Index

C

CIVIL RIGHTS.
Violation of civil rights of athletes, p. 222.

COACHES.
Appeals.
Touchdown and booster clubs.
Appeals on behalf of coaches, pp. 165, 166.
Contracts.
Termination of contracts, p. 6.
Dismissal.
Specifying rasons for dismissal, pp. 167, 168.
First aid.
Duty of coaches to render, pp. 208-211.
Medical treatment.
Duty to render, pp. 208-211.
Penalizing coaches for misconduct, pp. 234-237.
Transportation of athletes.
Use of private automobile of coach to transport members
of team, pp. 68, 69.

CODES.
Good Conduct Code.
Effect of violating on athletic participation, pp. 123-127.
Good conduct codes for athletes.
Generally, pp. 33-40.
Hair codes, pp. 34-40.
Training rules, pp. 40-44.

CONTRACTS.
Coaches.
Termination of contracts, p. 6.

COURTS.
Federal courts.
See FEDERAL COURTS.
Kinds of courts, pp. 11-13.